The Virtue in the Vice

Finding Seven Lively Virtues in the Seven Deadly Sins

Dr. Robin R. Meyers

Health Communications, Inc.
Deerfield Beach, Florida

www.hcibooks.com

Library of Congress Cataloging-in-Publication Data

Meyers, Robin R. (Robin Rex), 1952–
    The virtue in the vice : finding seven lively virtues in the seven deadly sins
/ Robin R. Meyers.
        p.   cm.
    ISBN 0-7573-0221-1 (hardcover)
    1. Virtues.   I. Title.

BJ1521.M57 2004
241'.4—dc21   2004047331

Publisher: Health Communications, Inc.
        3201 S.W. 15th Street
        Deerfield Beach, FL 33442-8190

Cover design by Lawna Patterson Oldfield
Book inside design by Dawn Von Strolley Grove

To Fred B. Craddock
Teacher and Preacher Extraordinaire

If my devils are to leave me, I fear my angels will take flight as well.

Ranier Maria Rilke

Contents

Acknowledgments

This book would not have been possible without the love and support of my family; the freedom of thought and conscience that defines the United Church of Christ; the countless teachers in my life, beginning with my father; the beloved pilgrims of Mayflower Congregational church, where grace hangs in the air every Sunday morning; my students at Oklahoma City University, who expect me not only to teach them, but to inspire them; and my soul mate, Shawn, who has loved me beyond deserving, and whose masterpiece is our children, marked with her face, and bearing even deeper the watermark of her tenderness.

It is also with real gratitude that I thank my hard-working editor at HCI, Bret Witter, who believed in this book and would not stop pushing me until it was the best it could be.

Prologue
The Virtue Is in the Vice, and Vice Virtue

Centuries ago, when most of us could neither read nor write, and there was a shortage of teachers and preachers, the church leaders got together and drew up lists of sins so people would at least know what *not* to do.

To help the average sinner understand the consequences they "classified" the sins. There were lightweight, middleweight and heavyweight sins. At the top of the list, in the super-heavyweight category, were the Seven Deadly Sins, which were "moral" or "capital" sins. They were toxic to the soul.

Some people think the list is in the Bible. It's not. It's a product of the medieval church and monastic thinking. According to the monks, who had plenty of time to ponder such things, the seven marks of complete separation from the saving grace of God were these deadly sins: pride, envy, anger, lust, gluttony, greed and sloth. This is the ultimate "DO NOT DO" list, which is why Hollywood loves it.

The church had an answer, of course, to the seven deadly sins: the seven "contrary" virtues—humility, kindness, patience, chastity, abstinence, liberality and diligence. This is the ultimate "TO DO" list, but movies featuring the seven virtues don't do as well at the box office.

Leave it to the church I love to oversimplify everything and to obsess on the *Thou Shalt Nots* (especially sins of the flesh) to the almost complete exclusion of the *Thou Shalts*— leaving us more fascinated by what is forbidden than encouraged by what is recommended.

To begin with, the Seven Deadly Sins are a strange mix of the juicy (lust) and the pathetic (sloth), completed by a rather sad parade of self-centered excesses and delusions (pride, envy, anger, greed and gluttony). The sins are more individual than collective, and they conjure up cartoon images: gluttony as a porcine figure with multiple chins dripping with sauce; sloth as a man unable to get out of bed, apathetically snoozing through life; lust as a wild-eyed and drooling lech, grabbing at the feast of flesh he cannot admire without devouring.

These caricatures seem so removed from everyday life that we stand and stare from a distance. We file past the rogue's gallery of big-time sinners like gawkers at the state fair, curious to see nature's biggest mistakes: the world's smallest woman, the three-headed calf, the gluttonously greedy.

The effect can be oddly reassuring, of course, because our own failures are thrown into perspective. Soap operas and daytime shock shows operate on the same principle. We may be miserable, but we're not that miserable! We may be sinners, but compared to the seven deadlies, we are strictly minor league.

Even so, the two most common questions asked about the Seven Deadly Sins are "Why seven?" and "Why this list?" The answer to the first is numerology, of course. Seven is a holy number (the number of days in the week, in creation, and "perfect" to Pythagoras—the sum of three plus four, both lucky).

The answer to the second question is more difficult. A closer look reveals nothing that is particularly hateful or vicious, what one writer calls "more the stuff of gossip and sitcoms than the target of moral philosophy." Nietzsche found many other vices in the human circus more "deadly" than these: cruelty, savagery, indifference to human suffering, tyranny, ethnic hatred, religious persecution and racial bigotry, just to name a few.

Consider, for example, the fact that drinking, and intoxication in particular, is not among the seven, even though it has undoubtedly taken a greater toll on the human family than any other vice. Could it be that wine played so central a role in both biblical culture and the ongoing sustenance of European monasteries that the monks decided not to bite the hand (or the grape) that fed them?

What's more, the Seven Deadly Sins deal so exclusively with gratuitous excess and dysfunctional ego that they fail to consider some of the most obvious and deadly of human behaviors: lying, cheating, stealing and adultery (which relates to lust, of course, but not seamlessly).

As for lying, moral philosophers once argued that telling a lie might be permissible in order to save someone's soul. Lest we forget, the term "propaganda" originated with the Roman Catholic Church's efforts to propagate the faith. As for cheating, stealing and committing adultery, these might also have an equally uncomfortable institutional resonance. Better to focus on the individual sinner and self-centered pathologies.

And why is murder not one of the Seven Deadly Sins, when it is considered the most unforgivable sin in the Judeo-Christian tradition? Is it because murder was sometimes sanctioned, as in so-called Holy Wars or the barbarism of the Crusades?

Even so, something else is even more troublesome here. By giving us Seven Deadly Sins and seven opposing virtues, the church is only adding fuel to a fire that seems to be burning out of control these days. We are living in a time of rampant and dangerous false dichotomies.

We want everything to be simple, clear-cut and unambiguous—especially in these dangerous times. In religion, in politics, in the ever-widening culture war, "you are either with us or against us." Under the guise of "moral clarity," a phrase as beguiling as it is dangerous, bullets fly across an ever-widening cultural DMZ—yet that's where most of us live!

A silent but troubled majority of Americans are increasingly uncomfortable with labels and increasingly disfranchised by the mass media's love of sound-byte confrontation and polemical entertainment masquerading as journalism. Most of us believe in both evolution and God. Many of us oppose abortion, but believe it ought to be a woman's choice. Millions of the faithful refuse to believe that the world can be so easily divided into good and evil, patriots and traitors, the born-again and the "left behind."

In a bumper-sticker world where the discourse of democracy is reduced to "America: Love It or Leave It," we are holding out for additional options. Some of us love America so much that its deceptions have become unbearably painful, yet we refuse to give up on its future. We want to stay and change it.

At the individual level, the Seven Deadly Sins and the seven contrary virtues are part of this same alien landscape. They are the costumes we wear to the saints and sinners' ball, but they are a masquerade. Real life teaches a far different lesson about the relationship between virtue and vice. Sin is real, and so are heroic efforts to live a noble life, but such a neat and simple polarity does not and has not ever existed.

Virtue is not the alien opposite of vice. It swims around in the same gene pool, beginning with the same raw material, the same appetites, the same universal human desires. Virtue and vice share a common nucleus, but they are formed differently. They are not opposites, but siblings.

This concept is not new. The Greeks understood, and our own life-experience confirms, that virtue is not just about following inflexible rules and making absolute moral pronouncements. Virtue is about acquiring a kind of inner compass, one that has its orientation from the intuitive habits of a lifetime. The academic world is showing a renewed interest in what philosophers call virtue ethics. This approach to right and wrong is based not on strict rules, but on the intuitive capacity of character.

With the rise of Christianity in the fourth century, virtue ethics was eclipsed by the church's emphasis not on wisdom, but on obedience. Humans could hardly be expected to determine right from wrong without help from God, which is why we call them the Ten Commandments, not the Ten Suggestions. The only problem is they are not that simple. "Thou shalt not kill" sounds unambiguous, unless of course you are at war, a supporter of capital punishment or about to put down the family pet. In the end, virtue is inescapably determined by context.

At work here is the law of unintended consequences. The more unrealistic we are about sin, the less realistic we are about virtue as well. Take the deadly sin of lust. We know that indiscriminate sexual desire can destroy worlds, families, friendships, even the priesthood. But is all sexual desire immoral? Celibacy may work for some people, but for others lust is merely driven underground, where it mutates into a shadowy thing, becoming dysfunctional and dangerous.

What about the virtue of sweet desire that accompanies real love? Can't one be in love while also lusting after the object of one's love in ways that are both compelling and sensitive, not to mention exquisitely insatiable? Come to think of it, the human race depends on it.

The six other deadly sins are plagued by the same artificial choices. In a time when more than half of all Americans are considered overweight and eating disorders are epidemic, we recoil at the sad compensatory obsession that is gluttony. Yet for millions in the Judeo-Christian tradition, no vision of the kingdom is more enduring than the feast. And what is the Eucharist itself if not a sacramental meal of inverse proportions, where eating less actually brings us closer to God?

When it comes to pride, considered by some to be the deadliest sin of all, we know that a blind, excessive and exaggerated sense of one's importance can lay waste to families and nations. This sin is also known as hubris, and the Greeks fashioned all their tragedies around it. But what do we mean when we tell our children to take pride in themselves, their work, their appearance, even in the essential goodness of their little souls?

The thesis of this book is not just a confirmation of Aristotle's "golden mean," where moderation is life's highest wisdom. Rather, this book asks the reader to consider a deeper wisdom, namely that the best things in life are the easiest to corrupt.

A sin is not just a matter of degree, but also of context. What is a drug, after all, but a medicine out of place? Why does one woman consider her old bedpost to be a piece of junk, while another woman considers it to be an antique?

This line of thinking can take us even further. If the best things in life are the easiest to corrupt, then there must be a converse logic as well: That embedded in the worst of things is a remnant of the best of things. Perhaps each of the Seven Deadly Sins harbors, in fact, a lively virtue.

After all, Satan is said to be a fallen angel, and the most beautiful and articulate one at that. Sin at its worst is a kind of spiritual apostasy. You take virtue for a joyride under false pretenses, promising to have her home by midnight, while knowing full well that you plan to rape her first.

In my twenty-five years of ordained ministry, I've found the church to be luridly fixated on sin and tellingly silent about virtue. What's worse, the average person in the pew is seldom instructed about the intimate and the insidious relationship between the two. We do battle with evil as if it were an invading force from without, rather than our own doing. We are deceived when we say that to be saved and sanctified is to be out of danger, when in fact it can mean that we are better equipped to do evil than before.

So let this be our common question and the purpose of this book: Is there a lively virtue that corresponds to each of the Seven Deadly Sins? If so, what is it? Can we reverse moral gravity and put the wings back on these fallen angels, restoring what was burned off when they passed through the superheated atmosphere of excess and depravity? If we can, then how do we live these lively virtues every day?

What if, instead of condemning the sin of pride, we could recommend the virtue of feeling worthy? What if, instead of simply condemning the green-eyed monster of envy, we could extract the essential virtue that causes us to want to emulate those we admire? What if, instead of warning against the consumption of anger, we could carefully differentiate between being mad and being possessed of righteous indignation?

What if, instead of the death spiral of lust, we could find a way to bring holy eros into the bedroom? What if, instead of shaming gluttons who eat too much, we could recommend a way of eating less and yet feeling more satisfied? The church calls it communion.

What if, instead of hurling epithets at the greedy, we could teach what is natural and healthy about wanting wisely? What if, instead of heaping burning coals upon the slothful heads of those who are lazy and apathetic, we could suggest the virtue of contentedness, which requires that we let some things be, in order that other, more important things might receive our full and healthy attention?

After all, what better weapon to combat the Seven Deadly Sins than their flip side, their alter ego—the Seven Lively Virtues? And what better way to confront the very same battles raging inside of us, given that we often know our demons better than we know our angels?

My fervent hope continues to be that contemporary theology might be rescued from its own cardinal sin: silliness. People are weary of confusing faith with the power of positive thinking. They are tired of hearing preachers "flap their gums about God," as Meister Eckhardt used to say. Most of all, we are all tired of false dichotomies. They divide us. They insult us. They keep us spiritually barefoot and simpleminded.

What we need is a list of virtues that make sense not just for saints, but for the rest of us. After all, our track record on sin is not too impressive, and we've tried just about everything. We've condemned it publicly while dabbling in it privately. We've tried to instill fear and shame, which has only made sin a better box office draw. We've railed against it so incessantly that, like Paul, we feel as if we might not have been so tempted to lust if someone had not been saying to us, again and again, "Do not lust!"

A better approach might be to do what a street preacher who worked with runaways and prostitutes once did. To one young woman who was lost and frightened he refrained from saying, "Shame on you." Instead he said, simply, "Don't you think you were made for more than this?"

Perhaps the most subversive thing that could ever happen to the Seven Deadly Sins would be for someone to walk up behind each one of them and whisper: "Don't you remember when you *were* more than this?"

Let's try it.

Chapter 1

WORTHINESS, NOT PRIDE

Pride goeth before the fall. No, pride guarantees it.

Anonymous

O nce upon a forgotten morning, in some forgotten room, amidst the refuse of poverty and despair, a sixteen-year-old girl from Cincinnati, Ohio, gave birth to a little boy without a name. She meant to give him a name, of course, but she just hadn't gotten around to it. There was no father to consult. In fact, she wasn't sure who the father was.

The hospital nurse came around to fill out the paperwork and asked the mother, whose last name was Maddox, to tell her the name of the child. "He ain't got no name," she said.

"Well," the nurse responded, "we have to put something on the birth certificate."

"Look, I'm tired," the mother said. "Can I go back to sleep now?"

So the nurse returned to her station, picked up a pen and wrote "No Name" on his birth certificate. That's what she wrote on that precious piece of paper, that legal tender that proves we exist, that coveted document stamped with inky little feet that goes into the lockbox and is cherished for all time. That's how his life began, this little boy. He came into the world as No Name Maddox. When his *teenage mother remarried, he became No Name Manson.*

By the time he was nine or ten, No Name figured out that his mother was a prostitute. Nobody told him this, at least not in so many words. But at night he would lie in his bed and listen to the sounds of his mother entertaining her clients.

Sometimes she sounded happy. Other times she sounded frightened. So No Name confused the two of them, and he still thinks that fear and happiness are somehow connected. As soon as he was old enough to make it on his own, he disappeared into the underbelly of the world and stayed hidden for a long time.

Then suddenly, out of nowhere, he surfaced, this time in the papers, on the West Coast. Only now he had a name, one that he had given himself and the press had passed along to the whole world: Charles.

Charles Manson. Running all over California, trying to kill his mother.

❦ ❦ ❦

Whatever went wrong here had nothing to do with pride. Not in the Greek sense of hubris, not in the Christian sense of self-idolatry. The truth is that the mother of Charles

Manson suffered from something much more common and much more deadly than excessive pride. She had a fatal case of worthlessness.

When the church fathers put together the world's most famous list of sins, the Seven Deadly Sins, pride always came first. It was considered the deadliest because it is the father of idolatry, and thus the mother of all other sins. The first sin for the Jews is first for a reason: "You shall have no other gods before me." That commandment includes one of the foremost temptations of all: to worship ourselves.

The English synonyms for proud include arrogant, haughty, conceited, egocentric, narcissistic, insolent, presumptuous and vain. The Greeks called it *hubris* (thinking oneself superior to the gods), which led to our downfall *(nemesis)*. Christians called it pride (thinking oneself independent of God or self-sufficient). Spinoza's definition may be the most precise: "Pride is thinking more highly of oneself than is just, out of love for oneself."

Described as a kind of deadly balloon, pride is an exaggeration of our own worth and power, and a thoroughgoing and often unconscious feeling of superiority to others. The well-known myth of Daedalus illustrates this idea. He was a master craftsman, and he made a pair of wings for himself and for his son Icarus, whose feathers were held together with wax. Daedalus warned Icarus not to fly too high, lest the sun melt the wax. But Icarus ignored his father's advice and ascended toward the sun. The wax melted and Icarus plunged into the sea. To be proud, in the classic sense, is to be out of place in the order of things, and not to know one's proper relationship to God.

The deadly sin of pride is self-consumptive, feeding on itself but never satisfied. Mental health professionals have actually taken the sin of pride to another level, calling it the basis of most emotional distress. A neurotic is by definition someone who is completely preoccupied with himself. The neurotic's navel is the center of the universe, and to look outside oneself is to look into a mirror.

But if pride goeth before the fall, as we all learned in Sunday school, then what happens when there's no pride at all? The problem with Ms. Manson wasn't too much pride, but none whatsoever. The only excess here is self-loathing. The only demon is a wretched feeling of inferiority. Instead of thinking too highly of herself, this mother proved that your children can actually inherit worthlessness. It can be passed down like blue eyes or dark hair. Worthlessness can curdle the cradle.

What's more, if you combine worthlessness with anger, you may end up with a psychopath. When Charles Manson's followers sliced open the belly of a pregnant Sharon Tate, he took the ultimate revenge against the power and peril of the womb. Perhaps at some psychotic level he was asking, *How dare women give birth to their sin? How dare they make money by ignoring their own dignity, and then abandon their mistakes like collateral damage?*

No, the problem here isn't too much pride. With all due respect to the church I serve and love, we are far more adept at warning the would-be sinner about what is deadly than we are at encouraging the would-be saint about what is virtuous. What's more, we aren't that all honest about the close and sometimes insidious relationship between the two. We know how to condemn depravity, and the feeling can be rather delicious. But we are amateurs at building up, at binding up, at peeling back the shame to find the child of God.

How many sermons on the Prodigal Son, for example, have been mostly spent describing what sort of activity constitutes loose living in a far country? Yes, yes—we all know it's Las Vegas. But by the time the sermon runs out of lurid gas, hardly an ounce of energy is left for the real miracle: the loving father. He is the one who, in his old age and on fragile bones, runs to meet the son who has disgraced him. The son was "lost, but is now found," was "dead, but is now alive." Without so much as a "Do you know how disappointed your mother and I feel?" he embraces the boy, who still smells of cheap perfume and pig slops.

So often in the church we are told, again and again, not to think too highly of ourselves. So we become walking, talking apologies for our poor miserable selves—and we think this pleases God. We stand around counting our shoelaces, refusing to take credit for anything because, after all, "We must be humble." This approach produces a lot of false humility, but very little in the way of healthy self-regard. We know the dangers of being in love with ourselves, but something else is just as bad. After twenty-five years in the ministry, I've discovered that most people don't even like themselves.

When it comes to the difference between virtue and vice, part of the problem is a language problem. We no longer use the word "pride" in its medieval context to refer to the idolatry of self, which is a sin indeed. Today "pride" is used interchangeably with "self-esteem." This rather pliable term is synonymous with "feeling good about ourselves," regardless of whether we have anything much to feel good about.

When we call pride a sin today we often confuse people, because in the current vernacular "pride" often means self-confidence. We tell our kids to "take pride in your work," and be "proud of yourself." When my kids were in junior high school, an assistant principal would come on the intercom every morning and exhort everyone to be filled with what he called "that Wildcat pride!" I was never exactly sure what that was, but felt fairly certain that a proud wildcat (as opposed to a humble one) did not push, shove, deface his locker or use profanity.

So in a semantic switch of sorts, pride, self-esteem and self-respect got all mixed up together in a kind of psycholinguistic soup. Modern therapeutic movements, which reached their zenith in the '70s, but whose conception of personal growth continue to this day, played fast and loose with the word "pride." Personal growth was often indistinguishable from self-indulgence. As for the people we hurt in the process of radical self-actualization, they would "get over it" as soon as they felt, you guessed it, "better about themselves."

What's more, feelings of guilt or despair are no longer interpreted as messages from God, signs to be read or marks of a lost covenant. They are merely temporary manifestations of low self-esteem. The higher our self-esteem becomes, the more insulated we become from the pain of broken relationships. Equipped with this bogus notion of self-esteem, a whole generation was taught to build the equivalent of psychic *moats* around our souls. Then we filled them with talking alligators whose language of choice is psychobabble. *If I hear what you are saying, it sounds like an attempt, which I reject, to allow me to be me.*

When I was in college, the reigning platitude was something I now consider to be a disaster: "I'm OK, You're OK." William Sloane Coffin Jr. may have been more on target, however, and expressed a more profound religious truth when he said, "I'm not okay; you're not okay; but it's okay."

Now, as always, the question remains: Where are we in this limbo between virtue and vice? We know that thinking too highly of ourselves is a sin, but so is not thinking highly enough. As my friend the rabbi put it, "A man who does not love himself will make a casualty of the neighbor sooner or later."

Perhaps the real truth is that the excessively proud person is really not in love with himself at all, at least not in a healthy way, but actually suffers from the opposite malady. My experience with people who seem puffed up with pride is that in fact they are excessively insecure. They are self-obsessed because they are still trying to prove something. They look down on other people because they have never really looked up to themselves. Hence, both hubris and insecurity are born of the same deficiency. We do not feel worthy.

Could the reason have something to do with homelessness? No matter how well sheltered we are, too many of us are spiritually homeless. We do not know where we came from, where we are going or to Whom we belong. We are named by our parents, but feel no kinship to the larger human family. We struggle to achieve recognition, but fail to recognize our own true identity. We live to be looked at and liked, instead of to be seen and loved.

In the meantime, the peace we so desperately want eludes us, because we are not at peace with ourselves. Moreover, despite all the proclamations to the contrary, a culture that claims to be peace-loving is not helping us. The truth is that American culture is not Christian. It is profoundly Roman. We worship perfection and power, and thus hate our imperfect lives and feel powerless in the face of impossible standards. These imperfections torment us, and our obsession with self-improvement leaves little time or energy for meaningful relationships. Beauty becomes form, not truth, and God becomes the ultimate critic. Then one day we look into the mirror and discover that by the impossible standards of the day, we are not the apple of anyone's eye.

Perhaps in our secularized pursuit of fulfillment we have struck an impossible bargain with ourselves. While the authentic language of religion tells us that we are as we *relate,* our society tells us that we are as we *accumulate.* What's more, when it comes to personal security, real or emotional, we are as we *insulate.* Just consider the explosion of walled neighborhoods, and tinted glass and the promise of safe passage through the corridors of privilege.

No wonder we are so unhappy. We are both estranged from others and unacquainted with ourselves! What looks like excessive pride is often just a form of compensation. Perhaps the "world is too much with us," as Wordsworth wrote, in part because we are on such unfriendly terms with ourselves. We "lay waste to our powers" because our souls lie wasted.

A noted theologian once said that there is no way to modulate the human voice in such a way that a whine becomes acceptable to God. But the whiners are everywhere. Excuse me for being such a constant disappointment, we say, but we were born for it. We are experts at qualifying accomplishment and second-guessing compliments. We are like possums, which as far as I can tell are embarrassed to be alive.

Is our pride born of spiritual amnesia? That is, have we forgotten the first premise of faith, which goes by the Latin phrase *Imago Dei*—made in the image of God? According to the Ephesians letter we are "God's masterpiece." We did not make ourselves, and so we can only be thankful for the gift of our lives. Gratitude, not belief, should be the first religious impulse. We are the mysterious intention of a mysterious Intentionality. God is in our DNA.

e. e. cummings tried to say this with his strategically jumbled poetry—that adoration is a child of faith, and both have their roots in wonder:

> *how should tasting touching hearing seeing*
> *breathing any—lifted from the now*
> *of all nothing—human merely being*
> *doubt unimaginable You?*

When the church warns us against the deadly sin of pride, we may be treating the symptom, but not the disease. What if more sin is born of self-loathing than self-aggrandizement? And what if the latter is really born of the former?

How strange to think that the answer to the deadly sin of pride might simply be a more authentic and natural love of self! As much as we might like a simpler approach to virtue and vice, the truth is that we can't just wad up sin and throw it in the trash, hoping to write about virtue on a clean sheet of paper. The virtue is *in* the vice, just as the vice is *in* the virtue. Sooner or later, we will have to dig sin back out of the trash, unfold it carefully, smooth it out on the desk of our minds and start writing something different on this badly wrinkled page.

If pride is always the first of the Seven Deadly Sins, then our first move in the search for Seven Lively Virtues is to strike the word pride and write in its place not self-esteem, but WORTHINESS. This was pride's given name, long before she developed doubts about her aging face in the mirror and started painting it.

Loving oneself is not the same thing as being *in love* with oneself. There is nothing to prove, because worthiness cannot be earned. It can only be recognized. Worthiness is a gift—not a derivative of being, but a constituent of it. Worthiness springs from creation itself.

Years ago, I was traveling to an academic meeting in the South. I stopped for breakfast at a small diner. When my order came, there was a small, milky-colored, grainy-looking pile of mush on one side of the plate. "What's that?" I asked the waitress.

"Them's grits," she said.

"But I didn't order grits," I said.

"You don't have to," she replied. "They just come."

That's the way it is with worthiness. You don't have to order it, and you can't do anything to earn it. It just comes. And that's what makes it sound so un-American. The Protestant work ethic demands that we earn everything—but isn't that what Luther was trying to help us crawl out from underneath, the impossible idea that we are ultimately justified by works? Of course, "faith without works is dead," but just as deadly is the illusion that one's worthiness can be earned or lost. The truth is, none of us could afford it, or find it.

Just imagine announcing at the opening bell on the floor of the NewYork Stock Exchange that you are "worthy." Then consider calculating your "net worthiness" at the end of the day when the gavel falls. Even if the market crashes, one's worthiness remains unchanged. Yet this notion scares people to death. We all have made a big investment in riding the roller coaster of guilt and shame; we would have to develop a whole new way of talking about one another. It would be nonsense to talk about what someone is worth if everyone is priceless.

After all, in an age when everyone has become his or her own self-help project, and bliss waits on the other side of an upswing in "bliss futures," nothing seems as incomprehensible as the notion of incalculable worthiness. Yet this is exactly what the writers of some old-time gospel hymns meant when they referred to all of us as "precious." That was no sugary compliment. It was theology.

Worthiness, at its core, is a religious idea, not because it is irrational (unreasonable) but because it is trans-rational (beyond reason). Like true beauty, which is best described as the "effortless manifestation of inner peace," true worthiness is the effortless manifestation of inner gratitude. Before I was the butcher, the baker or the candlestick maker, I was already something more important: a part of God's good intentions. I may have made mistakes, but I am not a mistake.

Just imagine, for example, what a dramatic change would

take place in our culture if more people felt not just good about themselves, but worthy? One of the most devastating and deadly realities in American life is our obsession with physical beauty as defined by the cultural standards of perfection. We live under an astonishing barrage of images whose message is, quite simply, "You don't look this good, but don't you wish you did?" Image is everything. Having a look is not enough. One must have *the* look.

What else can explain the fact that plastic surgery is the fastest-growing form of medicine? Under the heading "Is nothing sacred?" we recently witnessed the shameless reversal of one of our most treasured aphorisms. An ad campaign proclaimed: "Beauty IS Skin Deep." Was no one offended? Does anyone really care about the truth in this Orwellian age, or are we so busy searching for weapons of mass destruction that we fail to recognize an even greater threat: words of mass deception?

Take, for instance, the folk wisdom of native people who refuse to be photographed because they believe the camera can steal your soul. We discuss this in a tone of knowing condescension (poor unenlightened savages) while at the same time selling our souls to plastic surgeons. If you want to witness something truly sad, then study carefully the so-called "before" and "after" photographs advertising the face-lift as a remedy for the completely natural process of aging. The "before" pictures look like someone we know, even someone we love in all their "imperfection." The nose has character.

Facial lines are like the grain in seasoned wood. Crow's feet radiate out from eyes that have earned their stripes.

But the "after" picture represents something more than a mere transformation. Not only are the bumps and wrinkles gone, so is the person! It's as if in stretching the skin we have stolen the soul. He or she may look younger, but we almost feel the need to reintroduce ourselves.

Plastic surgeons, eager to perpetuate the myth that beauty really is skin deep, argue that with a change of look, some patients actually begin thinking of themselves as different people. Is this a good thing?

Or consider the Botox craze. These injections, advertised as misunderstood and meant strictly to enhance self-esteem, are turning us into a nation of zombies. After all, a paralyzed face has no character.

Again, if this counterfeit notion of worthiness is bestowed upon us by looking younger on the outside, then haven't we actually rejected the very nature of life itself? How else can one explain why people tell other people to "get real" while they are simultaneously paying a fortune for all the unreality money can buy?

In this Roman culture, we are obsessed not with beauty and truth, but with perfection. The mall is our citadel, and shopping is our national pastime. From the moment we set foot on this hallowed ground of ethereally packaged but profoundly useless stuff, our senses are bombarded by what I call the purveyors of perfection.

The message of every poster, every photograph, every window display is this: Beauty has become a form of iconolatry. To put it in the language of computers, shoppers look upon this virtual beauty from outside the proverbial window, even as they log on en masse to Madison Avenue's *Field of Dreams.*

Shoppers did not write the program. They are merely visitors, peons of imperfection whose searching carried them from the food court to the makeup counter. When they find the look they want, they merely point and click on the icon of their choice—using a VISA card, of course. For the right cash price, they might just *become* the icon, morphing into a made-over version of their old selves.

Most teenagers tend to think of themselves as nonconformists, as iconoclasts. They are mistaken. What they have become, ironically, are mass-produced icons. They are nonconforming conformists. They come in search of their "real" selves, but see nothing that is real. At a critical moment in their adolescent development, they search for what is authentic in a landscape of pure illusion.

In a persuasion theory class that I teach at the university, my students are always amazed to discover that even the models who adorn countless magazine covers with their fresh, come-hither faces don't really look that way. All magazine cover photos are "retouched" by professionals who remove wrinkles, pimples, stray hairs and other natural imperfections. So, in addition to the wonders of makeup, we perform a kind of photojournalistic plastic surgery. It produces not only a face we'd like to have, but one that the models themselves would die for.

On a recent visit to a movie theater in Edmond, Oklahoma, I strolled though a large suburban shopping mall. Such places strike me, more and more, as the most surreal and artificial of all environments. Not only have they become the modern equivalent of the biblical water well, a place to see and be seen, but they are also a place of profound loneliness. Plastic buying plastic. To walk through them is to journey through a media-controlled theatrical experience. The gallery is filled with gigantic images of young, beautiful human beings who exude self-confidence because they have "the look."

This is not Big Brother, but Blissful Consumer. They are smiling and laughing and looking carefree, but their ecstasy is not the result of inner peace. It comes from smart shopping. They have journeyed to Mecca, they have worshiped the brand name, and their salvation is obvious: They have perfect skin.

In the '60s, when a search for equality between the sexes brought us the first wave of feminism, people dared to suggest that women might just be equal and worthy by birth. A principle means of making the point was to insist that beauty is inherent—not stylized or coerced. But look what's happened now. We've gone from burning bras to the Wonder Bra, and women's magazines now offer advice on how to "develop your inner bitch." Lead articles in popular women's magazines give advice on how to win the race to be the most seductive and sexually talented, naming the "top ten things that will drive him crazy." The unspoken message is clear: You better, or some other woman will.

As a doctoral student in rhetoric at the University of Oklahoma, I was assigned to read the work of French philosopher Henri Lefebvre. He called the American marketing machine a form of "economic terrorism." At the time, I thought that phrase was a bit much, something you might expect from a Marxist who is just jealous of our prosperity. But the more I thought about it, the more accurate it sounded.

The older I get, and the more I interact with parishioners, colleagues and students, the more it seems to me that we are indeed "terrified"—in a constant state of anxiety because we don't look good enough, smell good enough or turn enough heads.

Kierkegaard called this angst, this inability to secure ourselves against our own insecurity, "the sickness unto death." Instead of trying to do what we can, where we are, with what we have (to quote Mother Teresa), we waste time on the impossible, wishing we were somewhere else and complaining that we never have enough. No matter how many beautiful things we buy, no matter how much we alter the body or change the face, the truth is that we live our lives unsecured and dying. We can rearrange the deck chairs on the *Titanic* of mortality, but sooner or later we hit the iceberg.

Even so, next to knowing that we are alive, knowing that we will die is the most important thing of all. In fact, strange as it sounds, next to life, death is the kindest gift of all. The child's wish is to live forever. Adults know that all meaning is derived from impermanence.

So the answer to excessive pride is not the opposing virtue of humility, because even this can be false, another form of self-centeredness. Some people, after all, are proud of their humility. Ministers are especially adept at garnering special recognition for their "modesty." After preaching a sermon on the subject of humility, a clergyman asked me what I thought of his sermon. In all seriousness, he said, "On a scale of one to ten, Robin, whaddya think?" I was tempted to say, "In my humble opinion, you shouldn't fish for compliments on a sermon about humility!"

Thus the "sin" of pride is not a matter of excess so much as a matter of deficiency. Pride is not so much a disease as a betrayal. The preacher who says to the prostitute, "Weren't you made for more than this?" is recommending not just a turning away from sin, but the recovery of a kind of *primal memory*. If we take the notion of worthiness seriously and believe in the doctrine of *Imago Dei*, then we would have to describe sinners in a whole new way. We would call them "traitors."

The important thing for us all to do, as we struggle to recognize the difference between the sin of pride and the virtue of worthiness, is to ask ourselves a crucial question: "What am I trying to prove?"

What is the *real* reason that I struggle to win the approval of other people? Is it because I have not made peace with myself? If my holy trinity is really me, myself and I, then what does it say about my understanding of worship and my devotion to something (anything) other than myself?

When I brag on myself, directly or indirectly, what does it say about my need to be recognized, or to be judged superior to others? If I am always looking down my nose at other people, what does my condescension say about the slumped state of my own soul? After all, what smaller package is there in the whole world than a person who is all wrapped up in themselves?

A very helpful distinction can be made between self-esteem and self-respect. Self-esteem has to do with evaluations of talent and merit; it depends a great deal on the standards of value in society and how one compares with other members of that society. But self-respect has to do with the inherent value and dignity of all persons and is, by nature, noncomparative. For example, being first-chair violin can produce self-esteem. But knowing the importance of the second chair, and feeling good about being one, is born of self-respect.

A second, equally important question is this: "Who tells me what I am?" To whom do I look, or from whom do I receive validation? Is it an acquisition or an inheritance? Was I born sinful, as the doctrine of Original Sin posits, or was I born good, as Matthew Fox's Original Blessing suggests? One can't have it both ways.

Human beings must either escape their fallen condition through salvation or claim their blessedness as a birthright. The former depends on adhering to doctrine. The latter can be achieved simply by loving oneself wisely and well. If the church, which invented Original Sin, can't tell us the truth, then we need to tell the church the truth. The Quakers are right. We are born good.

This belief puts us in good company, including the powerful verdict from Jesus of Nazareth, the central figure in human history. We are all worthy because that's how God made us. What God wants most from us is a worthy response to our worthiness, which means that our worthiness is inseparable from our ability to recognize the worthiness of others. It means we shall no longer consider anyone disposable, unredeemable or beyond the reach of grace.

When Jesus came upon a woman about to be executed for adultery, his first concern was for *her* (sitting with her quietly, he drew in the dirt), then with exposing hypocrisy ("Let the one among you who is without sin cast the first stone") and finally with making sure that she did not sin again ("Go and sin no more"). Why? Because she was made for more than this.

Everyone has the right to believe whatever they want to believe about the nature and purpose of religion, but I think its ultimate purpose is to train would-be traitors how to avoid the most fundamental form of treason. If God is for us, who can be against us? If we are made in God's image and likeness, and we breathe God's breath, then life is not a race. It's a promise not to forget.

When a woman who had a flow of blood for twelve years touched Jesus, he turned his attention immediately to healing her, because although she was Gentile, female and unclean, she was something else first. She was worthy.

When a blind man named Bartimaeus called out to Jesus from the side of the road, disrupting the triumphal entry into Jerusalem and annoying his disciples, Jesus stopped his own parade with two remarkable words: "Call him."

With an uncanny ability to be completely present to those who engaged him at any given moment, Jesus was also subversively perceptive when it came to the source of their sickness. If money, for example, had not meant everything to the rich young ruler, Jesus might very well have told him to write to his mother more often. Instead he told him to sell all that he had, give the money to the poor and follow him.

Concerned with the prattle that still passes for love of children ("They're the future, you know"), Jesus took a little one into his midst and made it clear that worthiness is not chronological. Everyone matters at every moment, no matter what their age, their beliefs or their wisdom. In fact, he implied that a certain kind of wisdom may even dissipate with age: "For to such as these [the innocent little ones] belongs the kingdom of heaven."

❦ ❦ ❦

*O*nce upon a forgotten morning, in some forgotten room, amidst the refuse of poverty and despair, a sixteen-year-old girl from Cincinnati, Ohio, gave birth to a little boy without a name. She meant to give him a name, of course, but she just hadn't gotten around to it. There was no father to consult. In fact, she wasn't sure who the father was.

The hospital nurse came around to fill out the paperwork and asked the mother, whose last name was Maddox, to tell her the name of her son.

"He ain't got no name," she said.

"Well," the nurse responded, "we have to put something on the birth certificate."

"Look, I'm tired," the mother said. "Can I go back to sleep now?"

So the nurse returned to her station, picked up a pen and wrote "No Name" on his birth certificate—on that precious piece of paper, that legal tender that proves we exist, that coveted document stamped with inky little feet that goes into the lockbox and is cherished for all time. That's how his life began, this little boy. If nothing had changed, he would have gone home as No-Name Maddox, and when his mother remarried, become No-Name Manson.

But that's not what happened.

Instead his mother fell into a deep, postpartum dream. In it, she was surrounded by water, and she tried desperately to keep herself afloat. She felt as if she were drowning. Men came by to help, one after another, extending their hands. She would reach out to them, but each one would step back, laughing.

Above her floated the child, the one with no name, the one she didn't really want. And yet the child looked different from everything around her. She was mostly submerged in darkness and despair, but the child, as if oblivious to her fate, was full of light. He seemed weightless and ethereal, and he hovered above her like the Blue Man in the Chagal.

The nurse's voice roused her from sleep, and the light of the child in her dream suddenly became the fluorescent light in the hospital room.

"Here is your son," the nurse said. "You need to try to feed him."

"Let me have him, please," she said, reaching out her arms.

When she took hold of him, he seemed weightless, just like in the dream. She smelled the fragrance of his head and saw his heart beating in the soft spot there. She looked at his perfect fingers and toes, and the way his ears lay flat against his head—and then he opened his tiny dark eyes and looked right at her.

That's when something happened.

She suddenly felt weightless too.

And not just from giving birth, but from shedding the past. Everything was different now. The child knew nothing about her.

Only that she was his mother, and for the first time she felt like one, bringing him to her breast.

She glanced over at the portable cradle and saw "No-Name" written on the blue tag and felt a quick panic.

He must never know, *she thought to herself.* I will name him Charles, after his grandfather. *He was the one man in her life who had loved her unconditionally.*

When the nurse returned, she commented on how well the young mother was nursing the baby.

"You mean Charles?"

"Is that his name?"

"Yes. Charles Milles Maddox."

"That's a beautiful name," the nurse responded, as she turned out the light. "I'll see that the birth certificate is done properly, and I'll come back in an hour to get Charles."

The two of them were left alone, and there was nothing but the sound of his breathing and that soft spot in his skull pulsing against her cheek. Mother and son. Kathleen and Charles.

New. Hopeful. Weightless.

Chapter 2

EMULATION, NOT ENVY

We seem no longer able to admire, respect or be grateful for what is nobler or lovelier or greater than ourselves. We must pull down—or put down—what is exceptional.

Henry Fairlie

S tanding before her third-grade class for the first time, the newly graduated elementary education major from Berkeley named Barbara could hardly wait to begin teaching. Steeped in the New Math, the New Grammar and the New Everything, she was persuaded by all the books she had read that her role in the classroom was strictly Platonic. She was the midwife who would bring forth the uncluttered brilliance that lay slumbering in the minds of every nine-year-old in her class.

She was determined not to be like the old teachers, who insisted on having their students memorize things, and recite great speeches, and study famous authors and thinkers as role models. She even had a name for this regressive pedagogy. She called it the "tracing-paper school." That's where children lay tracing paper over the great books and copy the works of others in their own hand.

So, after arranging the chairs in a circle and passing out a single sheet of blank paper to each child (asking politely that they not crumple it up, but assuring them just as politely that if they do, *that is their choice), Barbara the Brand-New Teacher from Berkeley said this:*

"Children, today we are going to write a poem. Does anyone know what a poem is?" A little girl squirmed in her seat and offered to break the silence.

"I think it rhymes."

"Very good," the teacher beamed, already feeling very midwific. "And what else do you know about poetry?" There was silence. "Have you ever read a poem before, or written one?" More silence. "Would you like to try?"

More silence, combined with sideways glances and shrugged shoulders that could only mean "Try what?"

Suddenly a little boy with dark hair and dark eyes thought of something very sensible. "Why don't you show us one, Miss Barbara? You could show us a poem."

"Yes, I could," she replied, "but I would much rather have you write your own, rather than trying to copy someone else's."

More silence. This wasn't an option that anyone had considered. That's when Miss Barbara launched into her carefully prepared speech about what makes a poem a poem—how it turns feelings into words, which when read aloud turns the words back into feelings. "Not a single syllable is wasted," she said. The children listened politely.

Then each child sat staring at the blank page trying to remember something that Miss Barbara said about words and feelings and all that. After all, they didn't want to waste a single syllable.

So they just sat there, frozen in a wasteland where none of us live: the land of abstraction. Finally, the little boy with dark hair and dark eyes decided to try again. He dared to speak aloud two of the most important and powerful words in the world. He looked at Miss Barbara and said, simply . . .

"For example?"

❦ ❦ ❦

Miss Barbara means well. She is protecting the autonomy of her students and teaching them to think for themselves. She wants to hear what they think, what they feel, what they might say if they were not intimidated by such oppressive notions as the right answer, the best word or the real poet. Granted, something is to be said for creative innocence, for the young mind as *tabula rasa*, for hearts speaking unfettered by convention or standards. After all, why copy the masters when you can be one?

This is a noble instinct, calling upon students to find their own words, their own voice, their own distinctive style. It's also akin to asking a brick mason to build a wall without a trowel or a level.

I teach public speaking to college students, and a few

students always try to imitate someone they admire, adopting a kind of alien "podium voice" borrowed from some rhetorical role model. In addition to not liking our bodies these days, most of us don't really like our voices either. So we go shopping for the right sound, much as we go shopping for the right look. One of my students actually said to me in class one day, "I need a voice makeover."

"Who would you like to sound like?" I asked.

Without hesitation he replied, "James Earl Jones."

Imitation, they say, is the sincerest form of flattery. The only problem is that if the words do not belong to us they make a distinctly hollow sound, as if the disconnect between someone else's work and our true selves is unmistakable. "We are not in search of someone else's voice in this class," I tell my students. "We are in search of *your* voice. We will study great speeches and great speakers, but not so you can imitate them. Rather, so you will emulate them."

During the semester, we watch a video of Martin Luther King Jr.'s "I have a dream" speech. Without fail, most of my students, for whom the civil rights movement is ancient history, are very moved by Dr. King's oratory. Most have never heard the entire speech and the way it builds upon itself with carefully crafted arguments dropped like pearls upon the necklace of repetition and refrain.

They hear the speech as an event, a "happening" in time and space that can never be repeated. They hear form and content, *logos* and *pathos* fused together perfectly. They hear a black preacher using religious language without apology, and citing the Constitution itself as a national text to critique America for failing to live up to its own scripture.

But most of all, they hear the power of metaphor, which is the highest achievement of language. And they hear that melodious crescendo—"I have a dream"—when Dr. King goes to preaching, as we say in the South. They become aware that although he says it over and over, he never says it the same way twice. With a cadenced inflection he walks the audience, one step at a time, up the rhetorical version of a stairway to heaven.

"Why do you think Dr. King has been called a 'rhetorical virtuoso,'" I ask the class, "since that's normally a word we use to describe musicians?"

"It's like he's singing," someone says.

"What do you mean?" I say. "Can you describe it?"

And then, as if primed by the power of metaphor, my students begin to talk that way. They emulate Dr. King, unaware: "It's like slow thunder and sweet rain . . . like a rolling river . . . like a man who, spiritually speaking, is acting under the influence."

There is, of course, always a student who just yields to the temptation to be jealous. "I'll never speak like that" . . . "Well, I'm no Dr. King!" And I say, "Of course not. Neither am I. But we can certainly learn a lot by studying his technique and adapting it to our time and place. Being prophetic is not just a matter of what you say, but how you say it and whether you are willing, as Dr. King was, to pay the ultimate price."

One day after I said this, the class grew very quiet. I could almost sense that someone was going to accuse me of putting Dr. King on too high a pedestal. After all, I teach in Oklahoma, and when I was only eleven years old, I asked two men in a department store to tell me who Dr. King was. One of them looked down at me and said, "Sonny, he's just a nigger, stirrin' up other niggers in the South."

Just then the resident shock-jock raised his hand, a frat boy whose eyes were always half shut from sleep deprivation and who wore the Confederate flag on his jacket. I nodded to him, not at all sure that it was a good idea. He said, with a kind of this-just-in smirk, "Well, I hear that the good reverend slept with white women."

In that moment the class got a glimpse of the difference between a constructive kind of envy, which causes us to admire and perhaps even emulate someone, and a destructive kind of envy, which makes us want to destroy them.

When the church called envy a deadly sin, it was nicknamed the "green-eyed monster." Envy is the pain we feel when we perceive another individual possessing some object, quality or status we do not possess. As a deadly sin, it's more than simple jealousy or passive resentment. True envy consumes us. If we can't have it, we don't want anyone else to have it either. Envy has a heart of darkness.

That's why everyone who writes about this deadly sin, from medieval moralists to contemporary secular humanists, describe it as something that "eats us up." Envy has a face that Thomas Fuller called the "squint-eyed fool." Words like "insidious," "gnawing" and "vampire-like" are used to described this complex human reaction to the good fortune of others (whether deserved or not). Its cousins are spite and sour grapes.

Where does it all begin? Envy begins in childhood, of course, when we are constantly compared to others. From the moment of our first conscious thought, we are immersed in a world that compares one thing to another in order to assign value. Are we smarter or dumber than someone else? More attractive or uglier? Are we stronger than the competition, or are we like the ninety-seven-pound weakling who is helpless when a bully kicks sand in his face?

In a sense, envy consumes us because it is essentially impotent. It hates what it cannot have or be, but has no plan of action that is not self-indicting. Shakespeare's Iago envies Othello's success and his beautiful wife, Desdemona. He hates the fact that a black, pagan Moor should be doing so well in white, Christian Venice. When Othello does not appoint Iago as lieutenant, he conspires to make Othello suspect that Desdemona is unfaithful to him. Iago succeeds in driving Othello mad with jealousy, and finally he murders his wife, who truly loved him.

Having deprived Othello of the object of his envy, Iago neither acquires Desdemona for himself nor brings anything but death and dishonor to all. Shakespeare, the master psychologist whose couch was the stage, put it this way: "If I, Iago can't possess the desired object, then Othello, neither will you." Samuel Johnson echoed the same idea, saying that most of the misery in the world "is inflicted by men that propose no advantage to themselves but the satisfaction of poisoning the banquet which they cannot taste, and blasting the harvest which they have no right to reap." Envy, said one philosopher, is a "loser's emotion."

It almost sounds as if nothing virtuous can be extracted from envy, the second of the deadly sins—unless, of course, we state the obvious and remind ourselves that envy is essential to our consumer society. After all, what drives capitalism is the urge to keep up with the Joneses. If they have it, we want it too.

But again, we must make a careful distinction between envy in its adolescent form (jealousy and petty resentment) and envy as a fully grown pathology. The latter makes us all into suicide bombers of sorts. True envy, as a deadly sin, has an inherently irrational quality. Things that are not really important become the objects of our obsession, as if they were central to our very being. Students experience pangs of envy at seeing a classmate make a slightly higher score on an exam. Someone else loses sleep over the fact that a friend is invited to a party, and she is not.

So instead of being inspired by the more intelligent student, or being content with the fact that no one gets to go to every party, some students actually try to bring down their classmates with gossip, or catch them plagiarizing so they can be turned in. That's why philosophers and theologians alike have compared true envy to hissing coals, poison spreading through the body, boomeranging arrows or a fire raging within. Envy almost always causes more pain to the envier than it does to the envied. An ancient Greek poet put it nicely: "Envy slays itself by its own arrows."

A lively virtue, however, is embedded in this deadly sin. The virtue grows out of the same soil but blooms in a completely different fashion. It is, if you will, a form of good envy that learns from greatness without wanting to bring it down. It's not an opposing virtue, as the church would say, but one that is mixed up with the same impulses that can lead to the green-eyed monster. This lively virtue, which has already been alluded to, is called EMULATION.

Though rooted in the same feelings that can grow into a deadly sin, emulation takes the acid of envy and neutralizes it with a nobler human response. There is no hostility, no secret desire to have the object of our envy fall from grace or be punished for their good fortune. In fact, this virtue, defined as "the effort or desire to equal or excel others," is an essential motivator for doing good, or at least for doing better.

Thomas Hobbes made this distinction long ago, but only to point out that emulation is not as consumptive and vengeful as envy. "Emulation," he writes, "is grief arising from seeing oneself exceeded or excelled by his concurrent, together with hope to equal or exceed him in time to come, by his own ability. But envy is the same grief joined with pleasure conceived in the imagination of some ill fortune that may befall him."

This distinction is helpful, but also begs a question: Must there be grief associated with our desire to emulate? I think not. As long as there are differences between us (and God forbid any other kind of world), there will always be judgments as to what is better, what is richer, what is finer, what is more appealing. Yet to be in the presence of excellence, virtue, bravery or enlightenment does not always produce feelings of sinful envy, or even disappointment that we failed to reach such a high mark. Sometimes we just wonder how this excellence was acquired, what part of it might be available to us or how we might be more like that which we admire.

When we meet someone who is possessed of great talent or great gifts, or who just seems to have an "enviable" amount of contentment and peace, we want to be more like them. We want to learn from them, to model ourselves after them, to live as they live. This desire is not sinful envy; it is good envy that motivates us to emulation.

If this were not so, then why would anyone choose teaching? The late Richard Weaver, a great professor of rhetoric, said once: "There are two postulates basic to our profession: the first is that one [person] can know more than another, and the second is that such knowledge can be imparted. Whoever cannot accept both should retire from the profession and renounce the intention of teaching anyone anything."

If a student of mine were to say to me, "I'm envious of all that you know," my response should be, "Good, can you stay with the feeling?" Perhaps in time the feelings would mature along with the student and turn into something more constructive. After all, since the beginning of time, the desire to emulate has given us the apprentice and the understudy. It causes the student to long for a virtuosity that is comparable to the virtuoso's. Emulation is not a sin.

Excellence is its own reward, its own source of constant astonishment. When I listen to Mozart's music, Maya Angelou's voice or Bishop Tutu's prayers, I don't feel the slightest tinge of envy. I am just amazed.

When I watch Mark McGuire or Barry Bonds swat home runs with a flick of their wrists, or Michael Jordan defy gravity, I don't secretly desire that they will fall from grace. When I hear the Boston Pops perform the *1812 Overture* in perfect syncopation with Fourth of July fireworks exploding over the Charles River, it doesn't occur to me to squint my eyes and wonder, *How did that lucky so-and-so get to be first-chair violin anyway? His father must have paid off a symphony trustee. I say we appoint a special prosecutor.*

What I am more likely to ask myself, however, is, *Why didn't I stay with my music lessons longer?* As for emulating Mark McGuire, or more so Barry Bonds, well, some things just aren't in the genetic code. On the other hand, I was mesmerized the first time I heard Maya Angelou speak, reading from her just-published book, *I Know Why the Caged Bird Sings,* and I took those lessons into my life as a public speaker. As for Bishop Tutu, I can't help but wonder, every time he smiles, why he isn't crying. How can he talk about forgiveness when he has witnessed so much that is unforgivable? His strength makes me stronger.

When I read the work of great writers, I am not envious of the authors nor their success. But I do find myself wanting to emulate those voices, to raise myself to a higher level of passion and eloquence.

Most parents would be frightened to learn how much more their children emulate them than learn from them. Since the beginning of time, young people have attached themselves to a teacher, a mentor or a role model of some kind. If envy was ever a part of a child's initial response to another person, it was not so much about having what they have, but about becoming what that person is.

In a previous book, I wrote about the high and holy art of parenting. I called parents the "big gods" and children the "little gods." Worship, I said, goes on in the temple of the home twenty-four hours a day. The little gods study the big gods, watching their every move, and their response to this worship is emulation. The little gods are, after all, just big gods in training.

The son will grow up to treat women as he sees his father treat his mother. The daughter will learn the graces of womanhood from watching her mother. The simple but frightening truth is that humans are formed in an envy/emulation spiral. We make examples out of ourselves, all of us, for good or for ill; we take our guidance and learn our lessons from the examples of others. We are walking, talking templates.

Again, the important distinction between emulation and mere imitation must be made clear. Imitation is a counterfeit form of emulation. Imitators do not take the time and energy required to learn what constitutes the soul of those they admire. They merely rifle through their bag of tricks, confusing technique with essence. Dressing like your hero, even talking like him, does not make you, in any sense, heroic. In fact, that "sincerest form of flattery" nonsense is just that: nonsense. Mere imitation is hazardous to your soul.

In my seminary days, I was fortunate to be taught by the finest teacher of preaching in America. His name was Fred Craddock, and I was so amazed by his style, his whimsy and his ability to wrap a razor-sharp intellect inside stories that were both folksy and spellbinding that I sought to imitate him in the pulpit. Try as I might, I could not be Fred Craddock. I could sound like him. I could even tell his stories, but it just didn't work. My wife had this figured out long ago, and she said to me once after a sermon, "Well, that was nice, but I was hoping to hear Robin today."

When I first heard Craddock speak, I truly envied him. But it was a positive envy, so at first I tried to imitate him. Now at last I have come to emulate him. Using all that he taught

me about language, about narrative, about the vital importance of sermons that actually walk the streets where people
live, I use the same tools, employ the same wisdom and
swear my undying loyalty to his inductive theories of human
communication. The difference is that now I tell my own
stories. I tell my congregation's stories. I tell the old, old
story. But I live more comfortably now, inside my own
rhetorical skin.

The relationship between envy and emulation is as complicated as it is commonplace. Take the Marlboro Man, for
instance (may he rest in peace after dying of lung cancer).
Open any magazine, and there he is, sitting astride a mag-
nificent horse, dragging a freshly cut Christmas tree through
a gorgeous mountain meadow muffled by newly fallen
snow. He is on his way to a tiny cabin in the distance where
his gorgeous wife waits with their scrubbed and radiant little
cowpokes. Here is life as it ought to be, we think: serene,
patriarchal, *au naturel.*

In fact, everything in the scene speaks of life, of evergreen,
with one notable exception: the cigarette. It is foul, addictive
and death-dealing, but somehow we miss the disconnect.
We want the lifestyle. We envy it, but we are not moved to
emulate. That would involve moving from the city to the
country and perhaps restoring a cabin in the mountains.
That would mean finding a Christmas tree to cut and drag
home, instead of going to the corner lot and paying a
fortune.

READER/CUSTOMER CARE SURVEY

BB4

We care about your opinions. Please take a moment to fill out this Reader Survey card and mail it back to us.
As a special **"thank you"** we'll send you exciting news about interesting books and a valuable **Gift Certificate.**

Please PRINT using ALL CAPS

Name _____
First   MI.   Last Name

Address _____

ST _____ Zip _____ Email: _____ City

Phone # ( ) _____ Fax # ( ) _____

(1) Gender:

_____ Female   _____ Male

(2) Age:

_____ 12 or under   _____ 40-59
_____ 13-19   _____ 60+
_____ 20-39

(3) What attracts you most to a book?
(Please rank 1-4 in order of preference.)

	1	2	3	4
3) Title	○	○	○	○
4) Cover Design	○	○	○	○
5) Author	○	○	○	○
6) Content	○	○	○	○

(7) Where do you usually buy books?
*Please fill in your top **TWO** choices.*

1) _____ Bookstore
2) _____ Religious Bookstore
3) _____ Online
4) _____ Book Club/Mail Order
5) _____ Price Club (Costco, Sam's Club, etc.)
6) _____ Retail Store (Target, Wal-Mart, etc.)

Comments:

_____

_____

_____

_____

_____

_____

So we settle for an accessory to the scene. We connect the cigarette to the lifestyle, even though the two have absolutely nothing to do with one another. That's as far as envy can take us. It's all show and no go. We look only on the surface, to what the famous person wears or what he smokes. Instead of considering what he is, we respond only to what he has.

That's why envy is a loser's emotion. Every road it takes us down is a dead-end. It has always been that way. One of the most remarkable discoveries that a serious student of the Bible makes is that in the New Testament more people get mad over God's generous treatment of those who don't deserve it than they do over God's harsh punishment of those who do.

In the parable of the eleventh-hour workers, the owner of a vineyard hires laborers throughout the day, then pays them all the same wage, including those who worked only one hour. The morning laborers were paid exactly what they were promised, but they resented the eleventh-hour workers. These guys had barely broken a sweat, and yet they received an amount equal to those who had worked all day and "born the heat of the scorching sun."

On closer inspection, however, we find that no one was mistreated; rather, some were over-treated. The owner's final question is as timely as it is poignant: "Do you begrudge my generosity?" The answer, of course, is yes.

The parable speaks to our inability to calculate the mercies of God. It addresses the problem in the early church of eleventh-hour Gentile converts to Christianity who caused resentment among the faithful at first, and then outright envy over their unmerited grace. But the parable is also a call to emulation. No, not the lucky workers who received a full day's pay for one hour of work, but the irrationally generous owner. Gracious to his workers beyond merit, the owner mirrors the graciousness of God to every human being, whether he has worked all day at being faithful or has barely broken a sweat. Our ways of measuring these things are not God's ways. Period.

On the surface, the workers seem jealous of one another, when in fact the one they most resent is the owner. His generosity toward those who don't seem to have earned a full day's pay creates the kind of envy that can become destructive. Human nature leads us to think that other people are always getting more than they deserve, while we assume that our rewards are just compensation. Destructive envy might well lead one of the all-day laborers to level the playing field by robbing one of his eleventh-hour brethren on the way home. Such an action could be justified on the grounds of fairness.

But the owner's question at the end of the parable is telling: "Can't I do as I please with what belongs to me?" He is, after all, being generous with his own money, not that of the laborers. So what would happen if, instead of sinful envy, the workers actually sought to emulate the owner? The eleventh-hour workers would be grateful for their good fortune and model their behavior after that of the owner. Having received beyond merit, they could choose to be generous beyond deserving. At the very least, they would buy the first round of drinks!

Seriously, this very idea—that having received beyond merit should make us generous to others beyond deserving—is the core of the gospel. The ministry of Jesus was, after all, not doctrinal. It was "commissional." That is, Jesus was not telling people what to *believe;* he was showing people what to *do,* and then asking them to go and *do* likewise.

Take one of the beatitudes: "Blessed are the meek, for they shall inherit the earth." This is not a commandment, and it would sound ridiculous if it were. Just try shouting, "We must all be meek!" Rather, the statement is a blessing, pronounced upon those who are already meek. But in this case, the world does not see it as a blessing at all. As J. Paul Getty famously said, "The meek shall inherit the earth, but not the mineral rights!"

The beatitudes are remarkable because the world has a completely different list, which is why the Sermon on the Mount (in which they were spoken) is the most radical of all social manifestoes. Jesus turns the notion of blessedness upside down and claims that the kingdom is populated by an entirely new cast of role models.

The disciples don't understand, of course, and begin to argue (in a case of preemptive interpersonal envy) over which one of them is the greatest. They still think that Jesus is headed for enthronement, and they are scrambling for seats of power around a table in the Jesus administration. Envious of the only kind of power they understand, they make green-eyed fools out of each other, like bored children in the back seat of a car.

In response to their ignorance, Jesus puts a real child by his side. "Whoever welcomes this child in my name welcomes me, and whoever welcomes me welcomes the one who sent me; for the least among all of you is the greatest."

Here is a call to reject the world's definition of power and status, and all the destructive envy it creates, and to emulate Jesus as a kind of anti-king. His teaching is full of action verbs and calls to emulate. He *takes* a child and *puts* it by his side. Then he calls upon his disciples not to argue like children, but to be childlike—to emulate innocence and vulnerability. Envy is all about power. Emulation should be about goodness.

The so-called new commandment itself is a call to emulation: "Just as I have loved you, you should also love one another." What's more, Jesus says again and again that just as he has emulated the Father, his disciples are to emulate him: "Very truly, I tell you, the one who believes in me will also do the works that I do and, in fact, will do greater works than these, because I am going to the Father." What will be the proof that the Holy Spirit is present with the disciples after Jesus is gone? That their emulation of Jesus matches his emulation of God: "As the Father has loved me, so I have loved you; abide in my love."

A strange and almost frightening passage in the New Testament is often overlooked. In it, Jesus equates his very presence as the example that removes all pretense of ignorance, and therefore all excuse for sin. In other words, you might not have known the one to emulate before, or how to do it, but there is no question now: "If I had not come and spoken to them, they would not have sin; but now they have no excuse for their sin" (John 15:22).

In Barclay's great work *The Imitation of Christ,* the title itself can be misleading. He isn't talking about imitation as the "sincerest form of flattery," but about something much deeper. He is talking about the emulation of righteousness.

The first person that Jesus may have emulated was John the Baptist. His emphasis on religion as compassionate action, not ritual obedience, may have been formative. When asked by the crowd in Luke's Gospel the simple and straightforward question, "What then shall we do?" John replied, "Whoever has two coats must share with anyone who has none; and whoever has food must do likewise."

When tax collectors asked John the Baptist the same question, he told them not what to believe, but what to do: "Collect no more than the amount prescribed for you." As if not to be left out of this new religious practicum, soldiers ask him also, "And we, what should we do?" And John said, "Do not extort money from anyone by threats or false accusations, and be satisfied with your wage."

After numerous examples of how to emulate specific behaviors, from shaking the dust of an inhospitable town off their sandals to doing as the Good Samaritan had done, Luke represents Jesus as defining faith as an emulation spiral: "Whoever listens to you listens to me, and whoever rejects you rejects me, and whoever rejects me rejects the one who sent me."

In essence, God's emulator wanted emulative disciples more than erudite ones. Jesus wanted followers, not fans, and he even warns his disciples not to think that he was the message, only the messenger. In one of the most stunning passages in the New Testament, Jesus takes a preemptive swipe at messianic envy: "Why do you call me good? No one is good but the Father."

From the moment of his first sermon at Nazareth, when he read from Isaiah and impressed everyone in the synagogue (what a fine lad he is, well-spoken too), the postscript was the part that almost got him killed. And what was it? That we must be doers of the word, and not hearers only, that religion is more than sweet incantation. There were, after all, widows and lepers who needed our help during the recent famine, and our apathy and hypocrisy have added insult to injury. Heaven has been sewn shut, for it has rained neither water nor mercy.

The most serious charge against Jesus was blasphemy, but what he did was even more offensive than what he said. "They were astonished at his teaching, for he taught them as one having authority, and not as the scribes" (Mark 1:22). The scribes had authority. What was the difference? Jesus taught by the example of his life. His listeners didn't know whether to drop to their knees and thank God, or to call the police.

Jesus' words were not from a new canon. This was a new incarnation, and this equal-opportunity emulation wasn't even copyrighted. When one of the disciples came to Jesus complaining that someone outside their group was casting out demons in his name (*don't we have a patent on this thing?*), Jesus said, "Do not stop him . . . whoever is not against us is for us." Then he said something remarkable, something that ought to give today's judgmentalists something to think about: "For truly I tell you, whoever gives you a cup of water to drink because you bear the name of Christ will by no means lose the reward" (Mark 9:38–41).

Apparently, the important thing is that the demons are cast out and that the thirsty get a drink of water, not that the right people get credit. Wondering who gets the credit is envy rearing its ugly head again, for which Jesus had an answer: "This is a way of life I'm showing you. I don't have a corner on the market, and neither will you. Compassion is its own reward, and discipleship is an emulation spiral. Emulate me," Jesus says, "as I emulate God."

Finally, as if to make certain that no one misunderstood on whose behalf this emulation should be directed, Jesus talked of a final judgment where the only criterion would be compassionate action. But he talked about it all in first person. Confused, his disciples asked, "Lord, when was it that we saw you hungry and gave you food, or thirsty and gave you drink . . . and the king [God's Emulator] will answer them, 'Truly I tell you, just as you did it to one of the least of these who are members of my family, you did it to me.'"

Envy is indeed a deadly sin. Envy caused Caesar to want to destroy the Christ child, and envy caused the religious leaders of Jesus' time to hate his popularity. But our response to remarkable human beings need not always take us down the path that leads to the green-eyed monster. Envy really is a loser's emotion, but emulation is a way for all of us to turn negative envy into positive emulation. Indeed, in the presence of greatness, not to emulate would be a sin.

In the end, the simple test for determining if the envy we all feel toward others at times might be redeemed is to ask, "Would I like to be more like that person? Or do I wish that person would fall from grace?" If envy drives us to hate someone or to wish someone harm, then it's a deadly sin indeed. Negative envy, in fact, is how people do themselves in.

But if this envy is born of admiration that leads to emulation, then it can make us more admirable. In a world that is starved for true role models, we are not talking about an insignificant matter here. This is no scholar's debate, nor some esoteric, intellectual footnote. We're talking about the very survival of virtue and wisdom. We're talking about how each generation avoids being orphaned from the truth. We're talking about how little gods become big gods.

The world is full of celebrities, but starved for heroes. Confusing the two is as dangerous as confusing envy and emulation. When we are asked to name the people who have made a difference in our lives, we almost always name a teacher, a family member or a close friend. These people did not make us jealous. We wanted to emulate them, even surpass them.

When parents talk about wanting things to be "better for their children than they were for them," they are not just talking about money. They want their children to be more, to feel more, to live more. Nothing pleases a real parent like having a child who actually excels over them in all these ways.

Just remember. Everyone is looked up to by someone. So if you and I are not worthy of emulation, then what are we good for? Anyone can teach the lesson, but some people *are* the lesson.

❦ ❦ ❦

*S*tanding before her third-grade class for the first time, the newly graduated elementary-education major from Berkeley named Barbara could hardly wait to begin teaching. Steeped in the New Math, the New Grammar and the New Everything, she was, nevertheless, not entirely persuaded that learning can occur in a vacuum, nor even quite as spontaneously as some of her professors had theorized. Platonic "memories" are fine, but for nine-year-olds, show-and-tell is even better.

She arranged the chairs in a circle, passed out a single sheet of paper, and told the students politely but firmly not to crumple it up, nor to start writing until she had given them permission. Then Barbara the Brand-New Teacher said this:

"Children, today we are going to write a poem. Does anyone know what a poem is?" A little girl squirmed in her seat and offered to break the silence.

"I think it rhymes."

"Very good," the teacher beamed, and then she said, "Can you think of a poem that rhymes?"

The little girl thought for a moment, and said, "I only know one, but you might not like it."

"Try me," the teacher said, smiling.

"I think that I shall never see a poem lovely as a tree. A tree whose hungry mouth is pressed against the earth's sweet flowing breast."

"Very good. And it does rhyme. Could the rest of you hear it?"

The class clown whispered something to his friend, and the two of them snorted out a giggle.

"What is it?" said the teacher.

"Nothing . . . it's not a poem really, but it rhymes."

"Try me," the teacher said smiling.

"At the table, my uncle says this for the prayer: Good gravy, good meat, good God, let's eat!" The circle erupted in laughter.

When order was restored, Barbara the Brand-New Teacher said, "Perhaps we should look at three different poems by three different poets." She proceeded to pass out three examples of verse, one each on three sheets of paper. One was a limerick, one was a love poem, and one was by e. e. cummings.

The class studied them carefully as Miss Barbara read them aloud. The limerick reminded the class of the silly prayer. The love poem was pronounced "icky" by an embarrassed student. e. e. cummings was judged hard to follow because he seemed to write his words out of order. Besides, said one girl rather ceremoniously, "He needs to learn to capitalize."

"Maybe he did that on purpose," said Miss Barbara, and the class fell silent, thinking it over. That's when the young man with dark hair and dark eyes looked up at the teacher and said, "Miss Barbara, have you ever written a poem? We'd like to hear one of your poems."

For a moment, she didn't know what to say. But then Miss Barbara admitted that she had indeed kept a journal once, and had scribbled her first poem in it when she was nine years old.

The idea of Miss Barbara as a third-grader stopped the class in its tracks. "You wrote your first poem when you were our age?" said one astonished student.

"Yes . . . it wasn't very good," she said, "but I didn't care. I just wanted to fool with words."

All of a sudden, the class became very interested in poetry, because the class was very interested in Miss Barbara. And Miss Barbara was a poet.

Everyone took out a sheet of paper, and for the rest of the afternoon, as rain fell against the windowpanes, they scratched out their very first rhymes. One little boy in particular, the one with dark hair and dark eyes, decided to use his own words, but not to capitalize anything. When asked about it, he said, simply,

"Just call me 'e. e.'"

Chapter 3

RIGHTEOUS INDIGNATION,
NOT ANGER

*Anyone who doesn't get mad at the right person
at the right time for the right reason is a fool.*

Aristotle

*S*he was an unknown seamstress from Montgomery, Alabama, and it was the first day of December 1955. There was no reason to believe this day would be different from any other day, especially for someone who counted for so little. She was a graduate of the Industrial School for Girls, a private school for poor blacks funded by liberal-minded women from the North whose motto was consistent with Leona McCauley's advice to "take advantage of the opportunities, no matter how few they are."

It was a muggy day, even for early December in the South, and Rosa was tired. The bus stopped to pick her up, and she climbed aboard slowly, choosing the nearest available seat at the front of the bus. It's a good thing she did, because the driver started moving before she even sat down, and the sudden motion threw her against the cracked vinyl cushion. To keep from falling, she grabbed the shiny metal pole that was slick with the oil of a thousand other hands.

He got on at the very next stop, and she noticed that he didn't remove his hat. His eyes were small, and his skin was red and blotchy.

There were no seats left on the bus, so he looked at Rosa and, without a word, motioned with one hand in a gesture that meant "Git up."

For some reason, she didn't move. And for a moment everything around her seemed to stand still, as if someone had taken a snapshot and then showed her a picture of herself, a portrait of her whole life in black-and-white.

She remembered going to sleep as a little girl and hearing the Klan ride by her house. She heard the sound of lynchings and tasted fear in the corners of her mouth. She remembered being afraid that the house would burn down. But for some reason, at this moment, she did not feel afraid. Not of him, not of white people, not of anything. She just felt tired.

I should not have to get up, she thought to herself. My feet hurt, and my back hurts, and I was in the seat first. How long, oh Lord . . . how long?

That's when she realized that she hadn't moved and hadn't answered him either. By now he'd lost what little patience he possessed. He looked at her with a look she'd seen so many times before, a look that said, "Move it, nigger!"

Time stood still, and she could hear her heart beating inside her chest. Part of her was angry, and part of her was frightened—just like always. Then, for some reason or for no reason at all except not to "make trouble," Rosa leaned forward and

*pulled herself up slowly and onto her aching feet. He moved
her aside with the back of his hand and sat down.*

*She rode the rest of the way home standing up, leaning against
one of those shiny metal poles that was slick with the oil of a thousand other hands. She was in the back of the bus.*

Sure enough, this day was no different from any other day.

🌿 🌿 🌿

1f the story had ended this way, the problem would not
have been too much anger, but not enough. Or at least not
enough of the right kind of anger. When the church called
anger a deadly sin, they were talking about what Horace in
the Epistles called a "short madness." There's a reason, after
all, that we speak of being burned up by anger: because until
anger's sudden fire is out, nothing around us is safe—
including those we love.

Anger is consumptive and usually does most of its damage
to the one who is on fire. Words like "blazing," "flaming,"
"scorching," "smoking," "spitting," "smoldering," "white-hot"
and "boiling" describe this inferno, which even the smallest
spark can ignite.

What's more, these often irrational explosions do not just occur among the temper-impaired or those who take anger management classes. Outbursts are a part of everyday life. Road rage is an epidemic in our time, and so is gratuitous violence. Both are directly related to a culture of hyperindividualism that seems to have placed a gigantic chip on everyone's precious shoulder. *How dare the world slow us down? How dare we be inconvenienced by a traffic jam, the slow pace of children and the elderly, or the inefficiency and ineptness of those who are clumsy?*

The ancient Greeks defined anger as that which is aroused when a person suffers a real or perceived injury and then takes action to punishing the real or perceived offender. Those feelings of anger are often intermingled with both pain and pleasure—pain at the injury and pleasure at the expectation of vengeance. To put a new twist on a popular bumper sticker, "I get mad, and I get even."

Needless to say, anger is all around us. The horrific events of September 11, 2001, created more anger in this country than any event since Pearl Harbor. In the days immediately following the terrorist attacks, the national mood was described as a "purple rage," and with it came an enormous outpouring of both patriotism and the need to retaliate against the real perpetrators, Osama bin Laden and his terrorist network. He would be "hunted down," "smoked out" and brought home "dead or alive." Anger causes us to make promises we can't always keep.

What's more, when dealing with September 11, the distinction between real and perceived injury becomes more than academic. Most Americans defended the war to drive the Taliban from power in Afghanistan and shut down their terrorist training camps.

The problem came when "perceived" injuries were ascribed to Iraq, and our anger was directed at a country which, although suffering under a cruel dictator, had done no real harm to us. We let our anger get the best of us, and only now have we learned that the weapons of mass destruction and links to al-Qaeda did not exist. We were right to be angry about September 11, but by focusing on our own desire for revenge we allowed ourselves to be dragged (some would say manipulated) into a war that has not brought us any closer to capturing the real terrorists. We were hurt, and so we lashed out. But the convenient target isn't necessarily the legitimate target. While our response may have made us feel better, it hurt our reputation around the world.

Meanwhile, in the hopeless situation that is the Middle East, suicide bombers, purple with rage, resort to their only means of making war. Their object is to kill as many innocent civilians as possible, to avenge the killing of their own. Then, in the purple rage that follows, a powerful army goes after the perpetrators with tanks, helicopters and bombs. The seeds of revenge are sown deeper and wider, and now even women are dying to kill.

This is why Dr. Martin Luther King Jr. called violence a "downward spiral" and why Mahatma Gandhi warned us that "an eye for an eye just leaves the whole world blind." Every day, we hear the gruesome reports of the latest attacks, followed by counterattacks. The average American used to be able to go for days without hearing a news report containing the phrase "body parts," but now suicide bombings are an almost daily occurrence. Such demonic anger endangers our very humanity.

Anger may be the most dangerous of all human emotions. A well-known psychotherapist who has written on the Seven Deadly Sins claims to spend more time helping clients deal with anger than with any other emotion. Indeed, much of the modern therapeutic enterprise involves the search for unidentified and thus unresolved sources of anger, which are then brought to the surface, hosed down and scattered like cool and benign ashes over a psyche that need smolder no longer. Getting rid of anger, we say, is always a good thing.

Even so, you don't have to be a social psychologist to know how much anger is out there. All you have to do is stand in line at the checkout counter. People seem ready to bite one another's heads off over too many items in the express lane, and they frequently look and sound pathetic doing so. Our fuse has become very short indeed, and our collective temper is frazzled.

When things don't go well, or we fail to get something we

want, someone else must be to blame. As a culture we are taught to assume personal responsibility, but as individuals we often act like victims. In pop culture, from cinema to country/western lyrics, it's the "Somebody Done Somebody Wrong" song, and we're MAD AS HELL AND NOT GOING TO TAKE IT ANYMORE!

Violent crime, at its core, is a manifestation of extreme and uncontrolled anger. So is the epidemic of abuse against children and spouses. So are bitter divorce proceedings and the endless litigation for pain and suffering. After all, if the popular bumper sticker is to be believed—"It's all about me"—then we invariably become an angry nation, full of combative idiots.

Poets and philosophers have known this for centuries. The central theme of *The Iliad* is the nature and consequences of Achilles' anger, and many of the stories and laws in the Hebrew Bible and the New Testament deal with both human and divine anger. So much so, in fact, that the monks decided long ago that anger, which could twist the soul into unrecognizable shapes and do untold damage, was not just a cardinal sin. It was also the outward manifestation of the other deadly sins, particularly pride and envy, and is regularly aroused by frustrated greed and lust.

"'Vengeance is mine,' saith the Lord." This ancient revelation is not so much about what God might do, but about what humans should not do. Anger that is motivated by selfishness will cause us to self-destruct. It will warp our lives.

As one writer put it, we all know someone whose "personality would collapse if it were not held rigid by resentment."

Even so, crucial distinctions can be made in the complex world of virtue and vice. Anger on behalf of others and anger directed at others—often as a way of feeding our own ego—are two entirely different things. Too often, when one of my students receives a grade that is lower than what she "deserves," she blames me for the failure. I was once accused of not "enabling" a student properly, or working hard enough to remove the barriers to her learning. Once, when a beauty queen on scholarship was enrolled in my public speaking course, she announced, somewhat indignantly, that she couldn't possibly be making a C in my course. When I asked why not, she said, rather ceremoniously, "Because I'm Miss Utah."

Human nature causes us to direct our generalized anger at a single person who becomes a symbol of all that's wrong with the world. Wrath needs an object and feels frustrated without it. After the Oklahoma City bombing, our anger was first directed against Arabs, and we immediately detained several men of Arab descent without cause, except that they looked to white America like terrorists. When the real perpetrator turned out to look very much like a clean-cut Marine, we found it difficult to believe that he acted alone and continued to spin out conspiracy theories like cotton candy. Anger can blind us and make us believe we know something, even when we know nothing.

One could even argue that anger needs an object and continues to look until it finds one. Perhaps the most psychologically disorienting event of the late twentieth century was the fall of the Soviet Union. We had so long defined ourselves in relation to the enemy of communism, as the all-important Other, that we turned inward to find new enemies: the government, environmentalists, feminists, secular humanists. As one noted theologian put it, "Wrath needs its enemy, it will create its enemy, it then nourishes its enemy."

Timothy McVeigh grew up angry and then left a loveless home to sojourn in a world of cheap hotel rooms, hate radio and the fraternity of racism. Failing to find himself worthy of love, he became addicted to hatred, which can be its own kind of narcotic. Perhaps hatred is the real deadly sin, but the monks decided to name its primary manifestation, which is anger, instead of its primary cause, which is fear.

McVeigh and his friends drank from the poisoned well of polemics and imagined a world of good versus evil. They saw nothing redemptive in their enemies and nothing evil in themselves. After all, you are either with us or against us.

When his homemade truck bomb brought down the federal building less than a mile from where I was teaching class on that fateful morning, he said he was avenging the botched and tragic government standoff at Waco three years earlier.

He also believed that his murderous act would signal the Second American Revolution as "patriots" poured into the streets and took up arms. Although he confessed to being unaware that a day care center was located in the building (where nineteen children were incinerated and then crushed), he apparently felt no remorse over the deaths of 149 adults. When asked about it, he referred to the unfortunate death of the children as "collateral damage."

No wonder the Spanish have a proverb to distinguish anger from vengeance. The latter, they say, is a "dish best served cold." Until anger has cooled, our best instincts are buried in a smoldering stew of resentment and self-righteousness. The same advice has been offered countless times by no less than the mothers of this world: "Don't write a letter to anyone while you are mad. If you do, put it in a drawer for three days, and then see if you still want to mail it."

To make matters more confusing, we are often told—especially in therapy—that there is "good" anger and "bad" anger. Just consider, for example, the fact that in psychoanalysis, unrestrained anger is in. But in churches, the notion that God could be angry is out. In fact, we are taught to vent and then say, "I needed that," while declaring adamantly that the notion of divine anger is a contradiction in terms. Karl Barth and Reinhold Niebuhr's crusade to bring back a legitimate concept of an angry God failed, and in most mainline churches, any anger attributed to God has been edited out of liturgy and sermon alike.

But if we are made in the image of God, then where did our "good" anger come from? I am just as offended as anyone by the notion of a vengeful God, but not quite ready to give up on the idea that biblical writers were expressing when they said that "the wages of sin is death." God isn't simply a divine scorekeeper who periodically calculates our sins and then punishes us. This notion—that God is a long-suffering, but not infinitely patient parent—was captured perfectly in a recent series of billboards containing messages attributed to the Almighty. One of them says, "'Don't make me come down there!'—God."

It's hard to imagine a more juvenile message or a more sacrilegious campaign. Apparently we are all teenagers facing the wrath of a God who has finally had it with our rooms, our friends and our loud music. If the prophetic tradition is to be believed, however, it is much more likely that God has had it with our selfishness, our cruelty and our lack of simple human kindness.

One does not have to believe that God is some sort of divine puppeteer, pulling individual strings to reward the righteous and punish the sinners. The situation may be something closer to the sentiment expressed in the language of karma: What goes around comes around.

Old Testament prophets understood this need to act to effect change and were far from dispassionate in their scathing critiques of the abuses of power. But it wasn't anger for themselves. It was anger over injustice. In that sense, the anger came from the very same well out of which love is drawn. Love for human beings produces a corresponding amount of anger over the abuse of human beings. For this reason, one of the most dangerous false dichotomies in religion is that faith can be spiritually redemptive without being socially responsible.

Besides, to assume that all human cruelty can and should be dealt with in a purely rational way, devoid of emotion and ashamed of righteous anger, is to disconnect the human heart from the hot blood of passion itself. We get angry sometimes because we care, not just because our feelings have been hurt.

Even though Seneca the Stoic argued that anger never has redeeming value, Aristotle argued for the very thesis of this book when he claimed that the virtue is in the vice, just as the vice is in the virtue. "Anyone," he said, "who doesn't get mad at the right person at the right time for the right reason is a fool."

What he is talking about is not explosive, irrational, misdirected anger, but RIGHTEOUS INDIGNATION, that smoldering sense that things are not as they should be, and that until we get angry enough about it, nothing will change.

The Danish philosopher Søren Kierkegaard spent most of his eccentric life trying to make the point that a huge gulf exists in life between concept and capacity. Good ideas don't change the world because noble sentiments do not make anyone more noble. Thinking the right thing should never be confused with doing the right thing, even though intelligent people make this mistake all the time.

The clergy are particularly susceptible to this. They are always preaching about love. They are always advocating love, explaining love and exhorting their followers to practice love. Surely, then, preachers are both loving and lovable, right? The problem here isn't as simple as practicing what you preach, although that's not a bad idea either. The problem has to do with being seduced by the notion that because you have preached, you have practiced!

The truth is, said Kierkegaard, that no one becomes a Christian by arguing for the advantages of Christianity or by hosting a study group on Paul over tea and cookies. No one becomes gracious by reading a good book on grace. In fact, life is not a theological puzzle; it's an existential opportunity. We are called upon to decide, and then to live with the consequences of those decisions.

To describe an authentically faithful person, Kierkegaard used words like "intensity," "discipline," "passion," and "pathos." What he feared most was that the gospel had become just a "piece of information," and discipleship had become a parlor game. "Our age," he said, "has sold its trousers to buy a wig."

Not much has changed. As the church fiddles, an American Rome burns with what Jonathan Kozol called "savage inequalities." The rich get richer, and the poor get poorer. We can't pay workers a living wage, can't provide affordable housing or a decent education, and won't even guarantee that all of God's children have access to medical care. We react to tragedy with ribbons and teddy bears, but feel little proactive indignation toward a system that manufactures human misery like an assembly line.

Part of our problem is that we know the sin of self-serving anger better than we understand the virtue of righteous indignation. *Saturday Night Live* gave us the caricature of the Church Lady, who is a cartoon of cool, detached, humorless piety. More and more people think that if you sit in a pew too long, you turn into a Valium Queen, a gossip, a shell of a human being whose religious affectations have turned her into a bloodless joke.

Yet the church has long recognized that anger for the right reason is not just permissible, but essential. The Episcopal priest William Stafford argues for a holy kind of anger that serves and protects something good:

> *As long as the cosmos throws up rebellion against God's goodness, there will be a need for right wrath. . . . In a sense, the love of social justice is this same anger transposed to a higher level. . . . The kingdom of God has not yet come, and until it does, anger is the right response to some realities.*

Even so, one has to wonder exactly what realities should be filling us with right wrath. Lots of people are mad, but not about anything that matters. What's more, righteous indignation seems all but lost in our genteel and politically correct mainline churches—even though the Scripture on which our faith is built is full of righteous rage. Abraham uses violence to rescue Lot from rival warlords. The Torah channels anger a thousand ways; Deborah routed Israel's oppressors in the days of the judges; the prophet Amos furiously damned the wealthy exploiters of the poor within Israel.

John the Baptist, who may have influenced the ministry of Jesus more than anyone, used vitriolic language against self-serving religious leaders. It is hardly coincidental that they both called their spiritual adversaries "hypocrites" and a "brood of vipers." Peter curses Ananias and Sapphira for their hypocrisy; Paul hoped that those people who forced Gentiles to be circumcised would slip with the knife and maim themselves.

Yet the illusion persists that Jesus was "meek and mild, gentle as a child." He loved children, of course, but because he loved them so much he cautioned about the fate of anyone who might harm them. Jesus said of people who would hurt children that it would be better for them "if a great millstone were hung around their necks and they were thrown into the sea." Perhaps today we would suggest that Jesus take anger management classes.

Selfish human anger is often as sinful as it is self-centered, but righteous indignation can be an instrument of the divine. The word "indignation" itself comes from the Latin root *indignitas*, from which we get the noun form "indignity"—the opposite of dignity. Hence, indignation is aroused not for injury to oneself, but in response to a fundamental injustice that denies dignity to others. Ironically, one must sometimes act in an undignified way in order to help bring down that injustice.

Perhaps we might consider a new way of thinking: If God is love, and love requires justice, then it might be more helpful to speak not of a God who is angry, but of a God who is indignant—burned up through us over our own injustices toward one another. The prophet Amos swore that God was furious. The truth may be instead that Amos was furious, which is how God restores dignity to those from whom it is denied.

Abolitionists like the Grimké sisters and Frederick Douglass brought a similar word to slave-owning America. God was about to "trample out the vintage where the grapes of wrath are stored," creating a wine of human blood. Sometimes the modern ear cringes at such metaphors. But their anger was right.

Conscientious objectors to the Vietnam War were not all cowards or communists. Some believed deeply that the war was both wrong and hopeless, and they burned draft cards as an act of righteous indignation. "Angry young men," they were called. Of course they were. Without passion, there is neither persuasion nor change. Without righteous indignation, the antiwar movement would have been nothing but a college elective, a dormitory discussion group, a coffee-shop dialectic where no one is right or wrong, just different.

Such is the tragedy of assuming that life can be lived as a kind of spectator sport, where a seat on the fifty-yard-line provides both the best view and the appearance of impartiality. Hovering above the fray has become a kind of social strategy—to abstain from voting and escape the messy consequences of making a choice.

Not long ago, a prominent United Methodist minister in my city faced a vote on the question of ordaining homosexuals. He knew that either way he voted tempers would flare. So he abstained. For this inaction he was praised by the church growth crowd as a "wise leader." What he is, in fact, is a coward.

"Never let them see you sweat" is part of the popular rhetoric of success. Detachment is the thing. Keep all your options open. But calm, cool and collected is not just a description of someone who is admirably under control. That description also fits someone who doesn't give a damn.

Kierkegaard, again, told us that an arranged marriage between the church and state almost guarantees a loss of passion. All parties speak well of one another but can't remember what attracted them to each other in the first place. It's akin to a husband who is constantly praising his wife to others, but in reality has forgotten the color of her eyes.

Half of all Americans today do not bother to vote. Having been born into a democracy, many of them feel entitled to opt out, or they have become so cynical about politicians and other liars that they put all their energy and time into private ambition. Meanwhile, in the world's newest democracies, the taste of freedom is so fresh, and the privilege of voting so exhilarating, that people will stand in line for hours and risk death just to cast their ballot.

For those of us who teach and live the life of the mind, it would be wise to remember that thinking can be just one more way to avoid living. Likewise, being only concerned for the poor, or troubled by the AIDS pandemic, or enlightened about the problem of the homeless changes nothing.

Yet in the halls of academia, Descartes's maxim—"I think, therefore I am"—has been twisted into a new shape: "I think, therefore I have acted." Pure cognition can save the world, according to this view; enlightenment equals transformation. But the right answer alone is not the right action. Sometimes everyone, including the best and the brightest, must take to the streets. The answer is not more people sitting in more ethics courses, but more people standing up to what is unethical and acting on their anger.

Although knowledge is good, it is not redemptive. Most business schools now require a course in "business ethics" (which students are quick to point out is an oxymoron). In fact, the number of ethics courses offered in American universities has exploded in recent years. What then are we to make of the fact that the corporate landscape is so littered with fraud, on such a massive scale, that the economy itself is threatened? From boardrooms to statehouses to the federal government, the American Way seems to be to take risks with other people's money, then plead ignorance or blame it on "creative accounting."

The great black educator, sociologist and historian W. E. B. DuBois was convinced that change in the condition of

African Americans could be effected by careful scientific investigations into the truth about blacks in America. As Dr. Craddock put it: "His research was flawless and his graphs and charts impeccable. After waiting several years and hearing not the slightest stir of reform, Dr. DuBois had to accept the truth about the Truth: it's being *available* does not mean it will be *appropriated*." That requires the passion of righteous indignation. In fact, the change that Dr. DuBois hoped for would not come until Dr. King marshaled anger into nonviolent, civil disobedience.

The fact that knowledge is not redemptive is part of the language of everyday life. Tell a friend to quit smoking because it's dangerous and deadly, and she will invariably say, "I know." Tell a kid to quit using drugs because it can ruin his mind and steal his future, and the kid will say, "I know." Tell a cheating husband to consider whether the affair is worth losing his family, his career and his reputation, and he will almost always say, "Of course not."

So here is the truth about the truth: the longest trip a human being will ever take is the journey from the head to the heart. The road to hell is paved with good intentions because good intentions have never changed anything. Something much more profound is needed: to act for the right reason, not just to think the right thoughts. This step requires passion, and passion cannot be disconnected from righteous anger.

This point was the fundamental premise of the so-called social gospel (as if there is any other kind): taking Jesus seriously meant engaging the principalities and powers on behalf of those whom the gospel was meant to free. Walter Rauschenbusch and Reinhold Niebuhr crusaded against the artificial separation of so-called beliefs and the will to transform a corrupt society. During his pastorate in Detroit, Niebuhr witnessed the birth pangs of collective bargaining in the automobile industry. He saw union leaders murdered for trying to improve the lives of people on the assembly line. Meanwhile, Henry Ford, who was widely hailed as a profoundly Christian man (he taught Sunday school and contributed handsomely to his church), was known to fire his workers, wait until hunger pinched their bellies and then hire them back at half their previous wage.

This dichotomy led Niebuhr to give us his enduring way of talking about *Christ and Culture,* and *Christ Against Culture.* Sometimes it is necessary for the good news to be inspiring, like leaven in the loaf, and sometimes violent and passionate, like the thresher who separates the wheat from the chaff. Christ is for us, but also stands against us when we are part of the problem.

This idea is a dangerous one, of course, for as St. Francis de Sales has reminded us, "There never was an angry man who thought his anger unjust." Take the angriest of angry white guys, radio talk-show host Rush Limbaugh. His vitriolic diatribes are laced with an anger that masqueraded as righteous indignation. His program was designed to fuel that anger and to give his ditto-heads their daily fix of liberal bashing. One of the most infuriating injustices, according to Rush, was the special treatment that rich and famous white males receive, especially Democrats, when they broke the law.

But when he was caught breaking the law and confessed to being a drug addict, it became clear, even to many of his fans, that mock anger can also turn us into hypocrites. He raged against the notion that personal misconduct should be protected by concerns for privacy, but then acted indignant when his personal failures became the subject of public scrutiny. Sometimes, what looks like righteous indignation is really just self-serving anger dressed up as "poor little me."

One early Christian controversy is illustrated by variant readings of a teaching by Jesus in the Sermon on the Mount. One version reads, "Anyone who nurses anger against his brother must be brought to judgment," while another reads, "Anyone who nurses anger against his brother *without good cause* must be brought to judgment" (emphasis added).

I believe that the second version is closer to the original, especially considering that Jesus himself is reported to have gone ballistic in the Temple one day. The so-called Cleansing of the Temple is one of the most remarkable stories in the New Testament. Unfortunately, cleansing hardly describes what went on there. As a child, I remember thinking that Jesus must have been doing some janitorial work, sweeping out the House of God. What else could "cleansing" mean? Now I know that today we would describe it, in the jargon of modern psychology, as "acting out." Jesus was mad as hell and not going to take it anymore, but he was not angry over some injustice done to him. Rather he was boiling over with righteous indignation over the corruption of religion in his time.

A scandal in the church today isn't that people don't believe enough of the right things, but that they hardly ever do enough of the right things. Jesus has become a cosmic pal dispensing life strategies, and the church has become a gift shop full of scented candles, trinkets and bumper stickers. God is wise, adorable or awesome, but never a radically disturbing presence. As for the Scripture, it has become as malleable as Play-Doh, and just as harmless to ingest.

This domestication of everything religious has driven out countless thoughtful and idealistic people who long for some connection between religious ideas and a sometimes savage world. They are tired of a politically correct God who is wise and adorable, but never frightening. As for Jesus, he has been transformed into something so pure and disembodied that we are all on the verge of being modern-day gnostics—people who actually argued once that the Lord must have "spiritualized" his food, instead of, well, you know, passing it along. Could it be that we are obsessed with the Second Coming because deep down we are really disappointed in the first one?

Gone is the man who became so angry he cursed a poor little fig tree for not bearing fruit out of season. Gone is the teacher of wisdom so incensed by the legalistic loss of true compassion in religion that his attack upon the Jewish purity system sowed the seeds of his own execution.

Conspicuously absent from the portraits of the gentle Jesus that hang in our churches is any notion that this man was dangerous, impulsive and explosive. Our images are so sanitized and pastoral as to make Jesus into the equivalent of a first-century Fred Rogers.

He got angry all right, but it was not self-serving. Instead he channeled his righteous indignation toward nonviolent change. Once, when his disciples begged him to bring a little fire down from heaven and scorch a few recalcitrant villagers, he refused. Some zealots among his disciples never went anywhere without a sword, and they seemed impatient with his commitment to nonviolence. Lest we forget, he lived in an occupied land, with swaggering Roman soldiers at the street corners and lots of angry people whose patience for "love your enemy" was all used up.

Anger is one of the Seven Deadly Sins precisely because in human hands it is almost always ambiguous. Even when we think anger is righteous, often it is not, as the Crusades and the perennial persecution of "heretics" has made clear. The denouncer of passions is himself enslaved by passions, and sometimes even the most well-known prophets among us have their own agenda—even if it's only a need to be widely known as a mad prophet, decrying the hypocrisies of our time. Nothing is more wearisome than a person who is professionally angry just to get attention, and yet nothing is more pathetic than a person who lives a life totally devoid of passion.

Without the right rage we can have little hope for real change in the world. The call of discipleship is a call to do, not a call to contemplate. There would have been no end to slavery without war, no civil rights movement without Bloody Sunday, and no progress toward inclusiveness in the church without bitter struggle and charged rhetoric. Even now, little hope exists for saving the environment until angry people realize that we all live downstream and we start marching upstream en masse.

In the end, there really is a simple way for all of us to know if our anger is right or wrong. When anger rises in the throat, ask yourself:

> *Is this for me, or for someone else? Am I turning red because someone has insulted me, treated me unfairly or failed to show me proper respect? Because if I am burned up on my own behalf, then my fate is almost guaranteed. I'll burn myself up. But if I am indignant over the plight of those who cannot help themselves, or who may have given up hope, then anger can be converted into perseverance, and perseverance will keep me on the long and stony road that leads to peace.*

The prophet Micah answered the essential question long ago: "What does the Lord require of [us] but to do justice, love kindness, and walk humbly with our God" (6:8). In other words, faith is a verb, and an action verb at that. Doing justice is inseparable from hating injustice, loving kindness cannot be separated from despising cruelty, and walking humbly with God still requires us to stand up and walk!

There may never be a more important time in American history to clearly differentiate between the deadly sin of consumptive, selfish anger and the necessity for righteous indignation. We are at war with terrorism and will be for generations to come. The manner in which we marshal our anger and wage this war will determine whether we make the world safer or more dangerous. National anger, smoldering beneath a fervent and even oppressive patriotism, can ultimately sanction the kind of indiscriminate rage that only breeds more terrorists. National indignation, on the other hand, moves deliberately but patiently to bring terrorists to justice, rather than bringing "justice" to terrorists.

Anger is truly a deadly sin, but righteous indignation is just as surely a lively virtue. Knowing the difference between them can make the difference between life and death. Anger may indeed be a "short madness," but a world without righteous indignation is left to go mad and then stay mad—all for a lack of the right kind of anger.

❦ ❦ ❦

*S*he was an unknown seamstress from Montgomery, Alabama, and it was the first day of December 1955. There was no reason to believe this day would be different from any other day, especially for someone who counted for so little, a graduate of the Industrial School for Girls, a private school for poor blacks funded by liberal-minded women from the North whose motto was consistent with Leona McCauley's advice to "take advantage of the opportunities, no matter how few they were."

It was a muggy day, even for early December in the South, and Rosa was tired. The bus stopped to pick her up, and she climbed aboard slowly, choosing the nearest available seat near the front of the bus. It was a good thing she did, because the driver started moving before she even sat down, and the sudden motion threw her against the cracked vinyl cushion. To keep from falling, she grabbed the shiny metal pole that was slick with the oil of a thousand other hands.

He got on at the very next stop, and she noticed that he didn't remove his hat, and that his eyes were small, and his skin was red and blotchy.

There were no seats left on the bus, and so he looked at Rosa and, without a word, motioned with one hand in a gesture that meant "Git up."

But for some reason, she didn't move. For one thing, her legs and her back were killing her, and this man had no right to order her around. It wasn't her mind that felt defiant, but her body.

For a moment, almost as if someone had taken a picture and held it up to her, she saw the entire history of white racism reflected like *a snapshot in those beady eyes. She saw her mother and father cowering in the dark as the Klan rode by. She saw burning crosses and the limp bodies of young men hanging from tree limbs with their heads cocked over in death and their tongues hanging out.*

That's when she realized that her hesitation had made him very angry, and he looked at her with that look she'd seen so many times before, one that meant, "Move it, nigger!"

And yet, for some reason, she did not move. She would not move. She would not be moved. And now she was feeling something like an anger of her own, but it was not the kind that burns you up. It was the kind that holds you up.

All of a sudden it felt wrong to move. All of a sudden she felt something like the "right" to stay seated.

And she was no longer afraid—not of him, not of anything. And so she stayed there. She stayed right where she was. She stayed seated.

And the whole world stood up.

Chapter 4

HOLY EROS,
NOT LUST

But virtue, as it never will be moved
Though lewdness court it in a shape of heaven;
So lust, though to a radiant angel linked
Will sate itself in a celestial bed
And prey on garbage.

Shakespeare, *Hamlet*

1t was the middle of the afternoon. He should have been at work, or perhaps calling on someone in the hospital. But instead he found himself seeking out, once more, the darkness of a movie theater.

Pulling into the parking lot, he looked for a space behind the theater where nobody would see his car—a green Ford Taurus the church provided for his pastoral duties. He found a well-hidden spot, put on a pair of sunglasses and walked briskly toward the front door. He hoped nobody would see him, but he could never be sure.

The place smelled of smoke and sweat and semen. Once inside, the contrast between the bright light of day and the near darkness of the theater blinded him for a moment. Until his eyes adjusted, he hesitated to move to a seat, fearing that he would bump into someone hidden in the blackness.

Standing at the back, he watched on the screen as a woman performed oral sex on three men standing in a circle around her. The soundtrack was always the same—perpetual moaning, not all of it convincing.

A handful of men sat spaced out in the darkness, like shadowy lumps of loneliness. They turned to look at him when he opened the door, because in a porno theater nobody likes the light.

He found a seat that put the most distance between himself and these strangers, keeping his head low and his eyes averted. This is shame's unwritten script, and as always, he felt deeply conflicted. For some reason, he both loved and hated this descent into mindless depravity. In part, he felt decidedly rebellious—as if he were having the last laugh in this uptight, hypocritical world.

Growing up in a parsonage, he had heard lots of sermons about the sins of the flesh. So many, in fact, that he wondered whether his addiction had its roots in excessive prohibition. After all, the Word had become flesh, and the church is the body of Christ, so why are we so paranoid about sex?

Perhaps orgies are really just the forbidden feast, the anti-Eucharist. Perhaps all this depravity is no more unreal than that of his childhood—the sterile, Styrofoam world of fellowship hall. Perhaps porn is humanity's true nature, stripped of its clothing, its pretense, its inhibition, its wearisome proprieties.

He settled in to watch the movie, knowing that, as always, there would be no plot. Just the hunger of bodies meeting and mating, and of fluids flying. Behold the celebration of carnal ecstasy with no emotional entanglement. Behold our culture's electronic offering to the god of lust. And behold the good reverend, finding himself both aroused and frustrated in the solitude of a secret life.

He felt alternately compelled and disgusted, and he wondered what his wife would think if she could see him now. Then he wondered: does she have the same animal instincts? Could she be like one of these women—all hunger and no conscience? The thought both excited and frightened him.

Then, as suddenly as the urge to come here had materialized, it disappeared—in a rush of spiritual nausea. He wanted out. He found the images repulsive. He could not leave the theater quickly enough, so he made his way back up the aisle with his head down again to avoid eye contact.

Once outside, squinting now in the light of the real world, he took a quick look around to make sure that nobody saw him. And then he told himself what he always told himself—that this was a waste of time and money. But most of all, he told himself that it was a waste of the trust that others had invested in him.

And he promised never to return again.

But it was a lie.

❦   ❦   ❦

Sometimes it seems as if sex is all there is, all that matters in today's culture. You don't have to be a prude to think this, or a repressive Victorian type or a self-righteous moral crusader. You just have to be alive, and not have your "eyes wide shut." It used to be that boys had to sneak a peak at

Playboy to feel titillated, but now all you have to do is maintain contact with civilization. From billboards to magazine covers to mainstream television, the message is pervasive: Sex is life.

We are supposed to be thinking about it all the time, maximizing our opportunities for it and always performing at the level of an Olympian. There is sex, and then there is everything else. And everything else we can do without.

The wise among us have always said that we ought to trifle least with that which matters most. If this is true, then we have almost guaranteed our own demise when it comes to human sexuality. Sex matters a great deal, and yet we do more than trifle with it. We use it to buy and sell everything, even if the mortgage requires our souls for collateral.

To begin with, we ought to be honest. Sex is the most powerful human hunger next to survival itself, yet it has now moved largely out of the realm of sacred mystery and into the realm of commerce. Prostitution may be the oldest profession, but human sexuality itself has now, quite literally, prostituted itself. Sex has become just one more commodity, and we pay for it one way or another. We also pay the morning-after price—in the currency of despair.

As a culture, we are generous with our bodies and stingy with our souls. We hunt flesh, but what we really crave is intimacy. Our addiction to sex is like our addiction to fast food: more of it never really satisfies, and it can be more than just unhealthy. In this sense at least, Freud was right. We display outrageously and obsessively that which we do not fully possess or have deeply at our disposal.

The age-old dance of seduction has become a game show, the national pastime, a compulsive form of validation. Once the "object" is conquered and compliant, it no longer seems quite so compelling—and so the game begins again. Look no further than the spate of so-called reality programs about dating and marriage, like *The Bachelor*. Women compete to be the most seductive, and the one who makes it to the altar is the "winner," which means, of course, that the show ends just as real life begins.

The result of viewing sex as recreation or personal valida-tion is all too obvious. Teenage promiscuity, rape, incest, pornography, prostitution, adultery, sexually transmitted dis-eases, unhappy marriages and divorce are rampant in our society. Tabloid TV features twelve-year-old children with multiple sexual partners, college athletes gang-raping a mentally retarded woman and the spread of HIV/AIDS by men who refuse to wear a condom because it decreases their sexual pleasure.

Jealous lovers commit murder, and embittered partners use sexual desire to manipulate and take revenge. Sex has become the primary weapon in the gender wars, instead of a uniting force, an ancillary of love. The deadly sin of lust, which is the unrestrained and unethical expression of the sexual impulse, is a destroyer of worlds. Whether it's ram-pant divorce, child abuse by the clergy or psychosexual violence that ends up killing the object of desire, lust betrays every good thing—especially trust.

A fair question to ask is whether things are really worse, or whether we just know more than we used to. I guess we can't really know the answer to that question, but this much is certain: the ancients had trouble defining lust for the same reason we do. The virtue of life-affirming sexual desire and the vice of amoral lust lie tangled together like lovers on the same bed. If our desire is satisfied in the context of love and mutuality, then we use words like "sublime," "ecstatic," even "heavenly." But if our desire is obsessive, predatory and self-ish, we use words like "disgusting," "perverse," even "criminal."

Marianne Williamson said once that lovers say "Oh God!" at the moment of climax because orgasm is the closest to God that some of us ever get. But when such desire knows no boundaries, disregarding all persons and all promises, it becomes the leading cause of betrayal and brokenness.

Someone said once that when bodies lie together they make an unspoken promise to one another. Either that promise is real, or it's a lie. And lying always destroys trust, the one thing that makes relationships and life itself possible.

Aristotle tried to make a similar distinction when he con-trasted the vice of licentiousness with the virtue of temper-ance with respect to the pleasures that arise from touch, of which sexual pleasure is the strongest. Touch can be a beautiful thing, and yet it can be abused. It can be gracious, reassuring and gentle, or it can be selfish. We all understand this, because certain hugs make us feel loved, while others make us feel uncomfortable.

In a culture that emphasizes instant, personal gratification we should not be surprised that sex has become the ultimate way to ignore the truth about consequences. Because the best things in life are the easiest to corrupt, the obvious corollary is that if sex wasn't so good, it wouldn't be so dangerous.

What's more, in the Western spiritual tradition we have succeeded, to our detriment, in separating body and soul. In much the same way we partitioned reason and faith, male theologians have given us centuries of paranoia and fear about the human body. We have been warned so often about the sins of the flesh that we have begun to wonder if that's all the clergy think about, or why it's the only thing they think about.

With our Western, mechanistic view of sex as a purely physical form of competition with winners and losers, no wonder we end up "using" one another like steroids. Bodies are advertised as objects-de-lust, and we go shopping for the model to maximize *our* performance. The ancient under-standing of lust as the indiscriminate consumption of the other for purely selfish pleasure had to do with physical grat-ification. Today, we have reworked the definition of lust to fit the age of narcissism. We seem more interested in what sexual conquest can do to confirm our own attractiveness and prowess. That is, our sexual addictions are more rooted in ego than in physical desire, and like Narcissus, every conquest is like a reassuring glance in the mirror. The only problem is that a single glance is never enough.

One theologian put it this way: "The man or woman who is consumed with lust essentially wears a sign that says, 'This property is vacant.' Anyone may take possession of it for a while. . . . It has nothing to give, and so it has nothing to ask." Some have even argued that promiscuity necessitates hypocrisy, promising more than it can deliver so that it can get what it wants without the sacrifices that intimacy demands.

That's why men lie to women so often, feigning affection in the world's oldest charade. "Men give love to get sex, and women give sex to get love" goes the old bromide—and it's not far from the truth. What may be yet closer to the truth is that men fake love to get sex, and women fake sex to get love.

Men are also taught, in myriad ways, to think that they cannot recognize and appreciate beauty without trying to possess it. The desire to possess is understood as a game played by the rules of seduction, and to the winner go the spoils of validation.

Men consider sexual conquest to be one of life's vital signs, proving that we are still young and attractive. In a memorable line from the movie *Moonstruck,* an older woman is asked by a younger woman, "Why do men chase women?" The answer: "Because they are afraid of dying."

Oddly enough, the message of most modern advertising is that sex appeal builds self-esteem, but in our society the opposite may be true. Beautiful women in particular learn to distrust compliments and to be suspicious of even the most ordinary acts of kindness. If they learn to protect themselves too well, they are called frigid. But if they don't build up their defenses, they are called by other names. In either case, the problem is always the same: how to bring body and soul together. Most poets, especially William Blake, said they cannot be separated. Blake wrote, "Man has no Body distinct from his Soul for that called Body is a portion of Soul discerned by the five Senses, the chief inlets of Soul in this age."

Meanwhile, the deep and widening sadness that hangs over contemporary culture is not made more bearable by casual sex, but less so. Television programs like *Sex and the City* give us as much unreality as possible, perpetuating the fiction that nakedness makes us vulnerable and real. Actually, people can lie to one another equally well whether they are dressed or not.

Make no mistake about it—skin on skin can be wonderful, even with the occasional negative consequences. But it can also make us feel that we have been consumed rather than transformed. In a sense, what promises to hook us up emotionally and spiritually ends up just hooking us up. And while we can argue in favor of sex the way we talk about beer (tastes great, less filling), the fact is that such an approach guarantees that sex will be as shallow as sports. What exactly is "anonymous sex," if not the ultimate oxymoron?

If certain bars are meat markets, then what does that make the patrons who go there? If one-night stands are so liberating, then why do some people need so many? The truth is that casual sex, although widely practiced, is itself a contradiction in terms. Even the most causal sex changes everyone involved. Such relationships are predicated upon the illusion that one can be physically intimate without being emotionally responsible. In the vernacular, we call that being used.

Yet if these statements are true, then what can explain our cultural obsession with casual sex and our reckless approach to physical intimacy? Are they reactions to Puritanical notions of human sexuality, where pleasure itself was suspect? Or are we so self-absorbed and competitive that we consider sex to be a right and our pursuit of pleasure to be a sport? Notice how often sexual conquest is expressed in competitive metaphors like "scoring," and how the rhetoric of sex dissects a woman's body from her soul, as when a man refers to sexual conquest as "getting a piece."

"We live in an age in which voyeurism is no longer the sideline of the solitary deviate," writes William May, "but rather a national pastime, fully institutionalized and naturalized in the mass media." Anonymous encounters online make it possible to have virtual sex—which is pure doublespeak, and where the triumph of the chat room is to make sex entirely a matter of disembodied eroticism, an exercise in solitude that masquerades as a relationship. "People now seem to have sex on their minds," Malcolm Muggeridge once said, "which is a peculiar place to have it."

All of this raises the legitimate question now before us: how does one recover a healthy and holy view of human sexuality from the sexual dysfunction of our time? For all our tabloid fascination with lust, and all the condemnation that religious communities heap upon this "depraved world," hardly a word is spoken in favor of the holiness of sexual desire, nor do we hear much in the way of instruction regarding sex that is virtuous without being prudish, appropriate without being unimaginative and morally authentic without being uptight.

Perhaps our religious traditions could help us? Maybe not. They are, at best, a mixed blessing. Orthodox Judaism, Catholicism and many Protestant denominations consider masturbation and sexual fantasizing to be sins. Jewish law severely restricts contact between the sexes and forbids men from listening to a woman sing (other than one's wife), lest they become aroused. The use of contraceptives is forbidden in Catholicism, and in many situations for Orthodox Jews as well. Religious teaching about sex, particularly in Christianity, often produces shame, guilt and sexual dysfunction.

After all, Catholic moral theologians have taught for centuries that even heterosexual intercourse between spouses is "impure" and must be "tolerated" for the purpose of procreation. The modern church has inherited this sad legacy, one that is wholly inadequate to address the problems we now face. People come to the church hoping for an affirming word, a word about the goodness of sex, and find blushing preachers whose sermons are as tepid as they are evasive. All we hear are warnings, which often have exactly the opposite effect. The apostle Paul confessed that he might not have lusted so often if he had not heard, again and again, "Do not lust!"

So what has the church offered us as the answer to the deadly sin of lust? The cardinal virtue of chastity. Where does that leave most of us? It leaves us out. What's more, it perpetuates a sexual schizophrenia that has marked the church's teaching from the beginning. The mantra of the church became that sex was an obstacle to the life of faith, never a conduit. We drag our bodies through life like a ball and chain, and we learn to loathe the very flesh which that same church claimed worthy to bear the incarnation. If the Word became flesh, then surely the flesh is not our enemy.

We have done a terrible job of helping people live comfortably inside their own skin. Instead of talking about a healthy sexual trinity, where humans beings are body and spirit, animated by soul, we have instead preached sexual dualism. These sermons take many forms, but the thesis is always the same: spirit good/body bad.

Just consider how we talk about the spirit. It is light, vaporous and disembodied. The body, on the other hand, is dark, earthy, odorous and bound to betray us. Its appetites are animal in nature, and thus the enemy of the spirit. Besides, the body soon rots away and is eaten by worms. But the spirit flies away, freed from its carnal captivity where it becomes, in some disembodied form, angelically asexual.

This pervasive conflict between body and spirit has contributed to the secret lives of so many supposedly virtuous people. When the news came out that well-known evangelist Jimmy Swaggart was visiting prostitutes regularly, people shook their heads in disbelief and chalked it up to the devil. After all, how could he preach such fiery sermons about human depravity, especially the sins of the flesh, and then get in his Lincoln Town Car and drive straight down to the red-light district of Baton Rogue to pick up prostitutes—one of whom accused him of soliciting sex from her twelve-year-old daughter? Perhaps his preaching was an attempt to exorcise his own demons? Perhaps he was preaching to himself?

Even so, blaming our sexual mistakes on the devil is not very helpful. Granted, he has done his job well as the fictional scapegoat for humanity's sin. But the tired cartoon of the angel and the little red man perched on our shoulders and whispering conflicting advice into opposing ears ("Be a saint . . ." "No, be a sinner") has only reinforced the idea that life is that simple. It also gives us the perfect excuse not to take responsibility for our own actions. "The devil made me do it" may be the most useful piece of religious propaganda since original sin. Either way, we just can't help ourselves.

It's odd, come to think of it, that when people do something good, something truly inspired, they rarely say, "God made me do it." The reason is perhaps all too obvious. We are happy to take the credit for our goodness, but eager to shift the blame for our mistakes.

Once, from the pulpit of my church, I said that if I believed in the devil, he would certainly love one thing above all else: simplemindedness. He would rule in the temple of either/or. He would offer courses on the myth of ambiguity and do battle against those pesky shades of gray. Worship would consist of pledging allegiance to a black and white flag, and there would even be a drive-up window for disciples to grab a few false dichotomies on the run.

Simplemindedness is, after all, how human beings end up doing great harm to one another. They are encouraged to be mentally and spiritually lazy, dividing the world into good guys and bad guys, the saved and the lost, saints and sinners. This approach has become the battle cry of many church people: the world is in a cosmic battle between good and evil. Goodness is a state of sanctification that comes from believing certain things about Jesus, and evil is the result of rejecting those doctrines and thus shedding their protective guarantees. Without the correct doctrinal armor, one is susceptible to the infectious ways of the devil, who is like a virus in search of a weakened immune system.

Meanwhile, when it comes to real life, most of us are

looking for an answer to a more complicated and realistic question: how can we be both erotic and faithful creatures?

Somewhere between the deadly sin of lust and the life-denying charade of chastity, there must be a lively virtue for lovers who are as faithful as they are frenzied. Because the truth is, when it comes to sex, what we need most of all is both a divine playfulness and a wholesome discipline.

Let's call it HOLY EROS—the kind of unblushing eroticism that is preserved in the biblical love poem called Song of Solomon, a song of pure ecstasy that overflows with anticipation, tenderness and the beauty of physical love.

> *How graceful are your feet in sandals,*
> *Oh queenly maiden!*
> *Your rounded thighs are like jewels*
> *the work of a master hand.*
> *Your navel is a rounded bowl*
> *that never lacks mixed wine.*
> *Your belly is a heap of wheat,*
> *encircled with lilies.*
> *Your two breasts are like two fawns,*
> *twins of a gazelle.*
> *Your neck is like an ivory tower. (Song of Solomon 7:1–4)*

Compare this sweetly explicit analogy of God's love to the story of David's adultery with Bathsheba, and the rape of his daughter Tamar by her half-brother Amnon, and we see clearly the difference between the virtue of holy eros and the vice of lust. David sees Bathsheba bathing, and he has her brought to his bed. Then he sets about covering his crime by putting her husband Uriah on the front line of battle, where he is killed. Amnon devises an elaborate hoax, feigning illness in order to get Tamar alone in his chamber. After he rapes her, he is disgusted with what he has done and banishes her. His brother Absalom avenges the rape, and more death follows. Lust takes what it wants, oblivious to the consequences, and thus sets death itself in motion.

Holy eros, on the other hand, is reciprocal and without shame. Just as lovers in the Song of Solomon desire one another, God longs for the redemption of creation. Desire is not inherently evil, unless it is inherently selfish.

Granted, the word "erotic" is a fallen angel in our time. It has come to refer to sexual acts, even to the lowest kind of sex, and is a popular name for adult bookstores and video arcades. But in classical literature it was *eros,* a highly spiritual, cosmic and lofty kind of love. In Greek literature, *eros* was the magnetism that held the universe together, and human love merely drew from this ocean of cosmic desire. Plato said of lovers that "the deepest insights spring from their love," and Socrates refers to himself as a lover. Jung said that "people think that eros is sex, but not at all. Eros is relatedness."

To combine the word "holy" and the word "eros" requires us to think of sex as divine, yet many people still find this to be difficult, if not impossible. Sexual desire is, after all, an animal instinct. But in the context of covenant and mutuality, sexuality is also a path to spiritual bliss. It need be neither tame nor impossible to control. It can and should be infinitely pleasurable. It can and does change with age, but it need not die. To the contrary, as we age we must become more soulful about sex, not less so.

Most healthy human beings can go through the motions of sex, even have an orgasm, and still not be fully present to their lover. What's needed, writes Thomas Moore in *The Soul of Sex,* is what he calls the "nymph of sex." By this he means that lovemaking can be a transcendent moment, as we learn from Aphrodite, because the soul is always in search of whatever will complete its desire. For this reason, ego is the enemy of spiritual sex.

In this sexually dysfunctional world, holy eros is the virtue we need, and it should be regarded, first and last, as a gift from God. As a gift, it recognizes itself as natural and normal, without using "natural" or "normal" as an excuse for excess. Holy eros is characterized by discipline first, and then by the abandon that discipline makes possible. As one philosopher put it, "Whatever diminishes constraint diminishes freedom." What he meant was that contrary to the premise of hedonism, boundaries are what intensify human expression. Poetry teaches this lesson by not wasting a single word. Fidelity to a lover teaches it also, through sacred sexual boundaries.

To illustrate the point, a rabbi asked all his students to explain the difference between a rushing stream and a stagnant pond. The answer, of course, is that one (the rushing stream) has banks that are closer together. Love that is narrowly focused is more intense. One can, of course, be intimate with everyone. But making the boundaries too wide only guarantees that one is truly intimate with no one.

Nothing need be timid, reserved or monotonous about sex in the context of a committed and faithful relationship. What makes holy eros possible, and the sex that flows from it so intense, is trust. In all areas of life, but especially in our sex lives, we hold back if we do not trust our lover. Ask anyone in a long-term relationship what regulates the quality of their sex life, and you invariably hear the word "vulnerability."

To the extent that lovers can open up and share their feelings about desire, they can also shed inhibitions and move toward a place where trust can dissolve fear and guilt, and where freedom takes on a whole new meaning. The space between lovers must be a safe place if it is to be sublime.

When honest, open communication in a trusting relationship is absent, people go looking for it, even at the risk of their most sacred promises. Most extramarital affairs begin not with overt seduction, but with authentic and self-disclosing conversation. Someone opens up, and someone else listens.

The real cost of infidelity, however, is not so much what has been given away, but what has been lost. Indiscriminate intimacy is a contradiction in terms, because what is bestowed elsewhere must be withdrawn from home. Holy eros, on the other hand, is a commitment to the beloved, not just a means by which a lover is satisfied or affirmed. Its intensity is made possible by honesty, which is made possible by vulnerability, which is made possible by trust.

Holy eros is qualitative, not quantitative, and yet nothing need be tame about it. It can be both feverish and not at all concerned should that fever subside or change. There are seasons to love, just as there are seasons to the body, and holy eros is not a numbers game. While we are constantly warned against the cooling of sex in long-term relationships, unmentioned is the changing nature of that sex. Couples who know each other intimately know that sex is not simply a matter of hydraulics. It is a form of communion.

Unfortunately, people have been taught to worry as much about how often they make love as the church worries about how often it serves communion. Yet, people who count the number of times they make love each week (usually as evidence to present to their beloved that it is not enough) almost guarantee themselves less sex, not more.

Those who embrace the virtue of holy eros, on the other hand, are physically intimate at an intuitive level, not at a competitive one. They can make love without even having sex because they understand the paradoxical wisdom of Kierkegaard, who said once that "silence also belongs to conversations at times."

Being tuned in to holy eros means giving your partner the space that he or she needs, that we all need, so as not to suffocate them. Lust takes what it wants, when it wants it. But holy eros is aware that great sex is not just a meeting of bodies, but a meeting of minds, or better yet, a meeting of souls.

In addition to all the recommendations for being attractive to one's lover and proficient when it comes to technique, we forget that in real relationships foreplay is not limited to what happens just before intercourse. Holy eros is a way of life, a commitment to beauty and truth, and an openness to the endless possibilities of pleasure. It knows better than to isolate sex as a single act, but instead understands it as the considerate life that periodically yields to spontaneous combustion.

Holy eros does not begin in the bedroom, but at breakfast with eye contact and genuine conversation. It continues with a phone call during the day just to see how the day is going, and it ends, not with a certain yes, but with the freedom to say no. Just as grace can only fill empty space, so too with holy eros. Without the freedom to say no (without guilt), there is no freedom to say yes and mean it. After all, nothing is more incompatible with good sex than the feeling that one is obligated to have sex. The twin enemies of holy eros are lack of time and fatigue.

Lovers ought to plan time to be together—time for intimacy and sex, and nothing else. We all need time for sustained and meaningful conversation. We need to listen carefully to the sound of one another's voice in a noisy world. We need to look each other in the eye. In the end, the most arousing of all behaviors in any relationship has nothing to do with "the look," "the move" or *Cosmopolitan's* "technique number twenty-nine." The biggest turn-on is *empathy*. The most effective kind of foreplay is consideration. The greatest gift is to really know one another.

Gifts and flowers ought to be "just because," not strategies for seduction. Lovers should remember that eros begins with the most practical of things, from physical affection that is not a prelude to sex to the fact that showers are good, but baths are better. Kissing is good, very good. Too often we quit kissing after we quit dating.

Also, holy eros brings back to the bedroom one of life's most important sounds: laughter. Possessed of imperfect bodies, non-Olympian technique and a propensity to be anything but seamless in our lovemaking, we laugh at ourselves and with each other. And in that laughter resides the music of the spheres. In that laughter lives the echo of the unconditional love of God reverberating against all our self-importance.

When the apostle Paul wrote that "Love never ends"—or to put it more positively, "Love abides"—he noted something that could easily be called nonsense today. Half of all marriages fail, and sexual infidelity is a primary cause of those failures. In one sense at least, a cynic might say that talk of love that "abides" is foolishness. On another level, though, where faith teaches lessons unavailable to the cynic, "love abides" is the most profound truth in Scripture.

Stanley Hauerwas, the resident provocateur at Duke University, said once that the most basic law of marriage could be stated in a sentence: "You always marry the wrong person." He goes on to explain: "The one you thought to be Mr. Right turns out not to be. Ms. Right tends to show up after marriage. But the adventure of marriage is learning to love the person to whom you are married. . . . Love does not create a marriage; marriage teaches us what a costly adventure love is."

Likewise, we often say, after years in a relationship, that we are "no longer living with the same person we married." Of course not. The other person could say exactly the same thing about you. People do not remain the same. They become new and different people, thank goodness—and that's why the choice of the verb "abides" is so important. When we stylize, stigmatize or commercialize human sexuality, it will invariably abandon those who know it only as the fever of youth. Holy eros does not belong to the young alone. It abides.

When we learn this, we can surrender gracefully the ways of youth and inherit something much more soulful. Less coupling and more couples will result. Perhaps even the church will overcome its desire to avoid the subject, as if hoping that it will just go away. Not talking about things, however, never makes them go away. It just guarantees they live underground, or above ground in a sadly mutated form.

As long as our theology remains schizophrenic, the same can be expected of the faithful. As long as we put sex and soul in different compartments, a deafening silence descends between them. One seems too kinky, the other too pious. But sex is too important to be blushed off the page or pushed to the margins of our common life. Richard J. Foster writes: "Sex in marriage should be a voluptuous experience. It is a gift to celebrate, excellent in every way. . . . Gladly we respond to the counsel of Proverbs: 'May her breasts satisfy you always.'"

Holy eros is good for a lifetime. It knows that age can add more in tenderness than it takes away in virility. It knows that anticipation, conversation and an almost sacred vulnerability in bed can take sex to a level not experienced in youth, or in what a friend of mine calls our "rabbit days."

With this lively virtue, everything about sex becomes more nuanced, more sophisticated, more subtle. Where we once submitted to the reciprocity of hormones, now we feast on the sweet alchemy of reciprocity itself. This is a sweet alchemy indeed. This is spiritual sex. This is holy eros.

❦ ❦ ❦

I t was the middle of the afternoon, when he should have been at work, or perhaps calling on someone in the hospital. But he found himself seeking once more the darkness of a movie theater that showed pornographic videos.

Pulling into the parking lot, he looked for a space behind the theater where nobody would see his car—a green Ford Taurus the church provided for his pastoral duties. He found a well-hidden spot, put on a pair of sunglasses and walked briskly toward the front door. He hoped that nobody would see him, but he could never be sure.

He reached into his pocket for a ten-dollar bill to pay the man whose face he could not see behind the glass. But instead of the money, he found a note in his pocket. It was a note that his wife had given him that morning.

It was a love note, scratched out on a textured piece of stationery with ragged edges, and the words were partly obscured by a lipstick imprint of her kiss, puckered into a red oval crease like the seal of a notary public.

He had forgotten all about it. She had handed it to him at breakfast, but asked that he "read it later." This wasn't exactly the "later" that either of them had in mind.

It was too dark to read the note, so he stepped outside for a moment, back into the lobby, back into the light, where he unfolded it carefully.

As he read the words to himself, he could hear the sounds coming from inside the theater, and it was always the same—perpetual moaning, not all of it very convincing. In that moment, he was aware of how sadly incongruent this was—reading a love note from one's wife to a porn soundtrack. Especially considering that the note was not just from his wife, but from the only woman he had ever really loved. It was a reminder that while he was away, she missed him and thought about him and looked forward to his return. It was, quite frankly, a rather bold bit of writing for the daughter of such respectable parents.

It was addressed not to "My dearest husband," but "To my Lover." And he read it once more: "I think of you every day . . . and it's not just your preaching I love, or your public persona. It's your skin, your shoulders, your hips and the way you move. I know that you have lots of important work to do, saving the world. But don't forget your 'homework.' And if you get a chance, a stolen moment . . . come to see me in the middle of day. Signed, Your wife and mistress."

He folded the note and put it back in his pocket. Suddenly, he was aware of the darkness of the place and the way it smelled of smoke and sweat and semen. The words of the note stuck in the back of his throat like a lump, like an epiphany in the strangest of places.

He was filled with shame and gratitude all at the same time.

Instead of buying a ticket, he walked out of the theater and back to his car, hidden from sight, just like this part of himself.

And he promised never to go back, but to go home more often.

And he kept his promise.

Chapter 5

COMMUNION,
NOT GLUTTONY

*For many live as enemies of the cross of Christ;
I have often told you of them, and now I tell you
even with tears. Their end is destruction; their god
is the belly; and their glory is in their shame; their
minds are set on earthly things.*

Philippians 3:18–19

*S*he always goes to the supermarket at three o'clock in the morning, because nobody will see her then, and she can wander the aisles undisturbed. She goes in the middle of the night because she hates the way she looks. But she hates even more the thought that she might be denied the one dependable and uncomplicated pleasure of her life: to eat.

She parks close to the door and walks in past the checkout lanes. There are the usual magazine racks, whose covers display the familiar gallery of thin, buxom women mocking her with their perfect bodies, dangerous cleavage and come-hither looks. It is a mosaic that declares our unofficial credo: you can't be too rich or too thin. It's the Barbie Doll syndrome, *she thinks.* And let's face it, the bitch gets anything she wants.

What I want, she thinks to herself, is a half gallon of chunky chocolate-chip ice cream and a two-liter jug of Coke. On the way to the freezer aisle she passes the bakery, looks at all the cakes, and tries to come up with a reason to celebrate. It must be somebody's birthday?

Next comes the candy aisle, where everything is supersized. You can't have too many Snickers around, *she thinks, and drops a dozen into what is fast becoming a pile of refined sugar wrapped in plastic. Vienna creme cookies, Pop Tarts, TV dinners—they all get tossed in. Finally, she makes it to the freezer, where the two-gallon twin pack of ice cream is the best deal. The best deal is always for the most food: "volume selling," they call it.*

On the way back to the checkout counter she looks into the basket and sees a million calories. That's when she remembers her most recent promise to herself to eat differently, to go on a diet and to get her weight under control. She knows this, but knowledge is not redemptive. Besides, what other pleasure does she have? The house is empty. The bed is empty. She is empty.

By the time she gets home it is four o'clock in the morning. She turns on the TV because the house is too quiet. She punches in the classic movie channel and finds an old black-and-white offering— something gauzy, romantic and therapeutically implausible.

She never makes it to the kitchen with the groceries, but drops the plastic sacks around the couch and props herself up on four large pillows. She eats until she can no longer taste anything. She eats to forget. One thing she's forgotten is what it feels like to be full.

At five o'clock she goes to the bathroom and wishes she could throw up—so she could eat a little more. She feels like a beached whale. She is bloated by fat, by chemicals, by despair. The movie is only half over, but she's lost interest now and decides to go to bed. After all, it will soon be morning, and with the morning

comes the light, the mirror and things she doesn't want to see.
   Mostly herself.

※ ※ ※

Y̶ou know this woman's name. It is legion. She has countless brothers as well, men who join her in living a shadowy, self-conscious existence. It may not be politically correct to say it, but while much of the world is starving, Americans are busy eating themselves to death. At last count, 60 percent of us are overweight, and the numbers just keep rising. Chronic obesity in children is an alarming public health issue. Physicians warn us, apparently to no avail, that the combination of high-fat, high-sugar diets with an increasingly sedentary lifestyle is to blame for a population that is dangerously overweight.

Meanwhile, there is a multibillion-dollar diet industry in place (some of it faddish, some of it fraudulent) to help us deal with the guilt and low self-esteem that comes from eating too much, too often. Yet despite endless new diet schemes, and any conceivable piece of exercise equipment available for three easy payments, we keep getting fatter. Is it genetic? Are we the victims of a sluggish metabolism? Or is it simply lack of self-control? In a twist on the ancient scriptural question: "Who sinned, this child's mother or father, that she should be born a slug?"

But never fear. There will soon be a pill to melt, block or dissolve the fat—"better living through chemistry," they call it. After all, it can't be our fault, can it? Who dares to call what we are doing a sin?

"Sin" would imply that we are somehow responsible. But in a culture of blamelessness, we assume that it's a genetic propensity, a slow metabolism or a sweet tooth that runs in the family. This explanation sounds much better than the truth, which is that most of us eat too much and exercise too little. What's more, chronic obesity may be more psychological and spiritual than physiological, especially in a culture that idolizes food.

Just consider what mass marketing does to turn a routine trip to the supermarket into a religious experience. Food is now packaged in such a way that we go out after things we need, yet come home with things we want. Impulse buying, they call it. My students were amazed to learn recently that crackers once came in a barrel, with a scoop, and no brand name. The modern supermarket, on the other hand, is the temple of excess, with music, lighting and an ingenious array of visual seductions—all designed to prompt us to buy more than we need, especially things we shouldn't eat.

Fast food is everywhere, available twenty-four hours a day

and uniformly bad. The drive-up window has become a kind of metaphor for the way we eat now. After giving the order, one is always asked to buy something else or something more, or to supersize it.

I ordered a small black coffee once, and added, "That's it," trying to stave off the inevitable pitch, only to have a charming youngster ask me if I wanted fries with that. In a moment of frustration I yielded to temptation and asked her the obvious question: "Does anyone you know eat fries with their coffee?" She said, "You'd be surprised."

No, I wouldn't. I'm not surprised at anything anymore when it comes to the way we eat, why we eat and how much we eat. Let's face it, the secret ingredient in all food now is cheese. Everything has cheese in it, and salt—which explains the popularity of cheese fries. (By the way, they call it "trans-fat" for a reason. It has the potential to trans-form you into a fat person!)

What has really changed is not our propensity to be gluttons, but our willingness to blame other people for it. In a highly publicized case, a teenager sued McDonald's for making him fat. The case fell apart when it was proven that nobody was forcing him to eat Big Macs every day.

Airlines must now try to figure out how much to charge a person who takes up two seats. The angry response from the nation's growing population of plus-sized people is to form advocacy groups. We teach our kids not to stare, and we avoid jokes that might insult those who are overweight.

These considerations are born of good and decent impulses. But they also mask the kind of candor we need to stop a serious and deadly problem.

When medieval moralists called gluttony one of the Seven Deadly Sins, they were doing something unheard of today: placing the blame for gluttony squarely on the glutton. He or she was sinning, and there was nothing funny about it. In fact, gluttony was considered not only a selfish form of hedonism, but a way of committing slow, self-indulgent suicide.

To be a glutton, clinically speaking, is to "eat to excess." But our reasons for doing so are as important to moral philosophers as the act itself. It is a form of self-obsession, a preoccupation with the pleasures of the palate, gullet and stomach. Gluttony is not only about eating too much, it is about eating for the wrong reasons. It is about a deeper hunger in the soul.

Such harsh judgments strike the modern ear as strange, even self-righteous. We live in a time when bodily pleasures are regarded as an entitlement, and anyone who thinks otherwise is considered a prude or suspected of being a closet hedonist. The whole idea of choosing to live a measured life, where less is more and austerity is a virtue, sounds almost subversive in our consumer culture.

But our choice should not be between the religious ascetic who feels guilty about experiencing any bodily pleasure and the hedonist who lives to do so. Despite W. H. Auden's maxim that "nothing succeeds like excess," the truth is that pleasure is qualitative, not just quantitative. Believe it or not, the quality of our pleasure is more important than the size of the plate on which it is served.

Even so, most people consider gluttony to be one of the least deadly of the deadly sins. Gluttony strikes us as sad, rather than deadly. What's a little overeating, after all, when compared to lust? What's a drooling beast, his face dripping with sauce, compared to someone consumed by pride, envy, greed or anger? The truth is that many ministers are overweight because in church gluttony is the one respectable sin. Congregations even take pride in how much their ministers eat, urging them to partake of multiple desserts while expecting them to stay in shape and cut a fine figure in the pulpit.

Yet when the first list of deadly sins appeared at the end of the fourth century, gluttony headed the list. The church knew what any of us can observe; gluttony and the other sins are connected. Overeating makes one less mentally alert, and the consequences of eating too much or drinking too much are all too apparent. Too much of a good thing is never a good thing.

What's more, gluttony is so closely related to lust that it often precedes it. There is often a feast of food before there is feast of flesh, as the debauchery of Rome made clear. The relationship between food and sex is as old as humankind, and Dante knew this. That's why he placed the gluttonous next door to the lustful in his purgatory. Likewise, any preacher should have no problem finding biblical support for the seriousness of this sin. After all, was it not an appetite for the forbidden fruit that cost us paradise?

Gluttony was also inextricably linked with sloth. Before we converted the medieval notion of sloth as *acedia* (a kind of demoralized, despairing stupor) into generalized laziness, sloth was understood to be the despair of the morning after. It was the hangover, the nausea, the heartburn and headache. Chances are you did not end up in bed with the object of your desire, but you almost certainly paid a price for your indulgence the next morning.

Gluttony was also thought to lead to pride, because food and feasts were a form of competition, just as they are today. What was at stake were bragging rights in a culture obsessed with the best, the richest and the most expensive trappings of wealth. Nothing has changed. Today, food is a status symbol, a way of proving that one has "made it." How ironic, when you think about it, that enough money is spent on one meal in an expensive restaurant to feed a poor family for a year, and yet overnight it passes into the same humble excrement as a bowl of beans and rice.

Does anyone feel guilty anymore, even the least bit, about what we spend eating out in this country? This statement is not meant to begrudge anyone the pleasure of a fine meal, but at what point does it become shameful? We claim to be overtaxed and underpaid—and so school children go without textbooks. Yet our national restaurant tab could fund them for a decade.

Remember, ethically speaking, that eating is a zero-sum game. The food supply at any one moment is finite. The more you eat, the less food is available to someone else. Our excess, and particularly our tendency to waste food, quite literally steals bread from the poor. And lest we forget, food is one of the principal means of distinguishing one class of human beings from another. Thus, the sin of envy makes its green-eyed appearance as well, as those at the bottom of the ladder must be content with the crumbs that fall from above.

In the biblical story of Lazarus the beggar, who lay in hunger and wretched poverty just outside the gate of a rich man's house, proximity to wealth meant nothing. The rich man's lavish table was close enough to cast a shadow over the beggar, but not a crumb fell from that table, and the dogs came to lick his sores. The two of them existed only a few feet apart, but they might as well have been living in parallel universes.

We often seem as oblivious as the rich man, indulging ourselves while millions go hungry. We walk down city streets on our way to the newest restaurant, making sure that we step over or around the homeless. We are offended if they ask for spare change, but we spend more on a bottle of wine than it would cost to feed and clothe them for a month. Gluttony is not just irrational. It is immoral.

And it is pointless. We expend all this time, energy and money on feasting, only to have the body convert these expensive delectables into the quintessence of disgusting:

vomit and feces. The object of our idolatry now becomes something far less glamorous, and our excesses can even be dangerous. One writer has even suggested that the deceased glutton be regarded and punished as a suicide.

The church had an answer for all this, of course—an opposing virtue. As the reader can guess, it was abstinence or temperance. In other words, better to do without, or at least to get by on as little as possible, than to run the risk of overindulging. Once again, the average person is left hanging.

The church needs to give us more than a warning about depravity coupled with the unlikely recommendation of totally withdrawing from our bodily desires. Most of us are left out of this false dichotomy. To illustrate the point, consider the implausible (some would say impossible) choice given to Catholic women between Mary, the mother of God, and Mary Magdalene. The former is said to be a virgin who gave birth with the help of the Holy Spirit, and the latter was incorrectly labeled a prostitute. Before the church "corrected" the error concerning Mary Magdalene (1,378 years later), the damage had already been done. In the minds of the countless faithful, the "two Marys" (virgin and whore) represented yet another example of spiritual schizophrenia—leaving most women out.

For men, the same paradox comes when looking at Joseph—the odd man in the crèche. There he is, looking on, the father who is . . . but isn't. Joseph was a man who may have influenced Jesus more than anyone, but who appears in the Bible as an extra and then disappears altogether before his son is baptized.

The truth is that the Seven Deadly Sins and the Seven Cardinal Virtues leave most of us hanging in a spiritual never-never land. Wouldn't it be much more honest to say that when it comes to food, abstinence is impossible, since we must eat to live? The same is true of temperance. Are we suggesting that something is basically wrong with food, so as little as possible ought to enter the body?

We have all had the misfortune of trying to cook and serve a meal to a finicky eater or someone who has lost the appetite for food. They turn their tepid appetites into advertisements for a discriminating pallet, or even offer it as proof of their gastronomic discipline. But the sad truth is that they may simply have lost their appetite—for food and for life. We are fond of saying that we "do not live by bread alone," but the truth is that a fine meal, lovingly prepared and consumed in the company of friends and loved ones, is one of life's great blessings.

Remember, in the New Testament the principal metaphor for the kingdom of God is a banquet, and Jesus once turned water into wine to keep the party going. On occasion, he is described as "reclining" as he eats. This signals the difference between an ordinary meal and a sumptuous, drawn-out affair.

What's more, Judaism advises moderation, but actually mandates pleasurable eating on many occasions. Food is considered good. When, in the Sermon on the Mount, the Lord is searching for a blessing upon those who have not lost their appetite for righteousness, he speaks of them as "hungering and thirsting" after it.

The highest and most sacramental form of eating in the church is not the potluck supper, but Holy Communion. In a world obsessed with having more and more, this ancient sacrament continues to teach a different lesson: Less is more. In fact, by a spiritual formula that is and ought to remain a mystery, Communion satisfies out of all proportion to size. Anyone who looks at the meager rations on the Communion table can see there is not enough. But somehow, there is always enough.

One does not have to be a Christian, however, to appreciate the lively virtue of COMMUNION. The difference, once more, is between quality and quantity. Whether we are connected to God in the Eucharist, or to the love of family and friends at home around a simple meal, eating can become more than just a refueling operation. We eat to live, not live to eat.

The virtue of food as communion does not produce a gaunt, pale, ascetic approach to food. Nor does it grant a godlike status to food, either as a compulsion leading to obesity or as a control issue at the heart of anorexia. Communion is an appetite for the fundamental blessing that is food—the way it connects us to the earth, to thankfulness, and to the author of every good and perfect gift.

Thus the opposite of a glutton is not a man who counts out beans on his plate and drinks water without ice. Nor is it the man who fasts and lets you know how much better the world would be if more of us practiced this ancient and noble discipline. The opposite of a glutton is a man for whom food is a means to an end, not an end unto itself. It is a woman who uses food and loves people, instead of loving food and using people.

Every parent knows the joy of seeing a sick child regain her appetite. It's a sure sign that good health has returned. To be hungry at the end of the day, and to prepare a meal and eat it with loved ones, is not just one of life's simple pleasures. It is life's most basic sacrament.

We live in a fast-food world of eating on the run or in solitary shifts to the beeping of the microwave. Sacramental living requires something else, something important. It requires a table—a heavy, solid table that needs polishing and can be expanded on holidays by inserting a "leaf" (my favorite metaphor for the kingdom). The table ought to sit unmoved and unmovable at the center of family life. Card tables don't cut it. TV trays are by definition "anticommunion" because they scatter people instead of bringing them together. As to eating while driving: this move advances neither civilization nor personal safety.

They say that love is a movable feast, but the table should be stubbornly inert. Its gravitational field should draw up chairs and hold them in a circle. Even the occasional human asteroid, wandering by, should find this orbit of food and conversation irresistible. We may not live by bread alone, but the truth is we can't live without it. Food is what brings us together, and food is what opens us to one another through conversation. Communion is what happens when pain and joy are served up along with bread.

For a glimpse of just how far we are moving away from the virtue of communion, where love enlarges and completes the meal, consider the average portion of food served up in American restaurants. If a little bit is good, then a lot must be better. But "all you can eat" really means more than you need, and people who gorge themselves on any good thing eventually destroy the goodness in it. Cleaning your plate, which has its roots in gratitude and in the virtue of "wasting not, wanting not," has become not only difficult, but hazardous to one's health.

This is the strange but impeccable math at the heart of the universe. Virtue and vice circle back upon one another and overlap again and again. The same food that brings life when taken and treasured in moderation brings death when not measured. "Too much of a good thing" is how we say it in the vernacular. That simple phrase contains more wisdom than we realize.

People who are familiar with the New Testament know that food played a primary role in the temptations of Jesus. The first of three tests in the desert was to receive bread, not by the fruit of his hands, but by magic. This temptation was to become an economic messiah—to be able to feed the world. Anyone who thinks this temptation was not real has made a cartoon of the gospel and forgets that the sound of hungry babies crying in the night would have tormented Jesus most of all. Besides, a temptation can only be called a temptation if the outcome is not a foregone conclusion. To be tempted means there is a real chance that one might yield to it—even if the one being tempted is Jesus. His answer: "It is written, 'One does not live by bread alone, but by every word that comes from the mouth of God'" (Matt. 4:3–4).

At stake here is not the morality of hunger and the means of satisfying it, but rather idolatry—the sin that Israel recognized as the mother and father of all other sins. The First Commandment forbids having "any other gods before me." That includes food, even for the hungry and destitute.

Indeed, when Jesus declines the tempter's invitation to partake of food, even to feed his own hunger, he reverses Adam and Eve's decision to seize the fruit offered to them to make themselves like God. From the beginning, food and its proper place in human life are at the heart of the new covenant.

Other biblical characters were not so resilient. Esau sold his future in God's promise for a "mess of pottage." Israelites in the desert craved the leeks and garlic of Egypt while complaining bitterly about manna. Leviticus listed hundreds of unclean but popular foods that would leave the people of God unable to approach Yahweh in priestly worship.

Some have argued that what sounds like an unnatural preoccupation with food and spirituality was really just a religious rationalization for common sense. In a time before refrigeration, food had to be prepared and stored very carefully, as a matter of life and death.

But that's not all there was to this ancient concern for food and its relationship to faith. Having a theology of food was, and still is, important.

Now that the teachings of Jesus have freed millions of us from a legalistic concern about what to eat (it is not what goes into a person that defiles, but what comes out of the mouth), we are in even greater danger of not keeping food in its proper context. Freedom from legalism does not equal license to indulge with an Epicurean obsession.

Communion is a theology of food, a celebration of the sacrament of eating together—both moderately and joyfully. It is not the food we love, but the way that love completes the food. The ancient act of offering a toast is a manifestation of this virtue. At the table of mutuality and respect, one does not belly up to the trough and begin to gulp and slobber. One recognizes the moment, raises the glass, looks present company in the eye, and with words of hope and encouragement converts nourishment of the body into nourishment for the soul. It is not just what we eat, but why we eat and with whom we eat.

Just think how often the glutton eats alone and in silence. Those who share food in communion, on the other hand, must pass what is on the table before helping themselves. There is an unspoken rule that the portions must be adequate for the number of guests present, lest the food run out before all are served. So we start with small portions and discuss the leftovers later. We take turns chewing and talking, but are warned not to talk with our mouths full. The table has its rules, its common courtesies, its turn-taking, sacramental ways. Eating becomes a social experience.

Now, a thoughtful reader has the right to ask: What about the person who must eat alone, and often does so? Can food can be considered communion when no one else is present? How does one "commune" when it's a table for one?

Eating alone can also be a sacramental experience. The food is still a blessing, and the spirit of God is the unnamed table guest. A prayer before a solitary meal is just as important as one offered in the company of friends—even if nobody else is listening. The virtue of communion requires thankfulness because praying before a meal is not just a social custom. Prayer establishes the meaning of food and the unmerited grace of its availability.

Having something to eat, anything to eat, reminds us that we are among the privileged in the world. If we wolf it down like an ungrateful animal, we insult the giver of the gift. Food is not morally neutral; it is precious because it sustains what is precious. Millions and millions of human beings do not have enough food, and for lack of what we routinely abuse, even children shrivel and die.

For this reason, I am always impressed when I see a solitary diner bow his head for a moment of silent prayer before eating his meal alone. Many outward displays of piety make me uncomfortable, but not this one. After all, if we only pray when other humans are present, then for whom are we really praying?

Once, when Lyndon Johnson asked his press secretary Bill Moyers to say a prayer aboard Air Force One, the young Moyers, who was a Baptist minister, bowed his head and began speaking softly. President Johnson, in his booming Texas twang said, "Speak up, Bill, we can't hear you!" To which Moyers responded, "Mr. President, I wasn't speaking to you."

All of this reminds me of an obscure Old Testament passage that I first encountered in seminary. In it, the rabbis advise us: Never curse a deaf man. *How strange,* I thought to myself. *I mean, if he's really deaf, then where's the harm?* Let's say you're having a bad day, and a deaf man walks by and you decide to lay a few expletives on him—just for the satisfaction of getting it off your chest. What difference does it make? He can't hear you.

Now I know what the rabbis were saying. It's true that he couldn't hear you. But you could hear you, and God could hear you. And two out of three is enough.

People who no longer visit their elderly mother or father in the nursing home will often say, "She wouldn't even know that I was there." But you would know that you were there. And God would know that you were there. And two out of three isn't bad. The truth is that each of us is what we do when no one is looking.

A popular saying holds that you are what you eat. That's true. But you are also *how* you eat, *why* you eat and *how much* you eat. How you eat reflects the vanishing art of table manners. Holding a fork properly and instructing children to eat with their mouths closed and to finish one bite before shoveling in another is not a remnant of old-fashioned propriety. These lessons are testimony to the importance of respect: for food, for oneself and for others.

Why you eat reflects the place of food in your life. We should eat when we are hungry, and not just to pass the time or compensate for boredom. Eating when bored may be the principal cause of obesity, even though it doesn't change anything. If you were bored before you ate, you will still be bored after you eat. So at the very least, we've got to stop asking food to do the impossible, like make us happy.

Regarding how much you eat, bingeing is a psychological and spiritual affliction, not a physical one. If you consistently eat until you are miserably full, and if you must medicate yourself frequently because of your eating habits, then your body is trying to tell you something. If you feel guilty not cleaning your plate, or if you find yourself cleaning up other people's plates, then you are eating for the wrong reasons.

Our bodies are healthy when they are in balance. Health is homeostasis. If we were to adopt a more Eastern way of eating, we would concentrate on balance instead of quantity.

We would find satisfaction in less, knowing that more is not always better.

But above all, we would recognize that the most powerful antidotes to gluttony are community and thankfulness. These qualities turn eating into communion. Communion is what turns the table from a trough into an altar. Instead of just refueling the body, eating becomes a celebration of the miracle of food itself—connecting us to strangers and to the earth.

When we unwrap a loaf of bread, we should remember: a stranger grew the wheat, a stranger milled it into flour, a stranger baked it and brought it to market. Unlike the Little Red Hen, however, we should not assume that our lack of involvement in the process means we do not deserve the bread, nor are we obligated to share it. It is all a gift, like life itself.

In my experience at the table with both rich and poor, I have noticed one thing again and again: those who sit at the most sumptuous tables almost never say grace. The more they have, it seems, the less thankful they are. The ritual of picking the right wine has become more important than the rituals of gratitude. But then, in all honesty, what would we say? "Thank you, Lord, for granting me the wisdom to pick the right wine in a world of culinary ignorance, and to make the right statement with this food in a world that begs bread"?

The rabbis have a saying for this: "Anyone who eats a meal, however humble, without thanking God is little more than a thief." We could go even further. Those who worship food itself, or use it to fill an aching void in their souls, are not just thieves, but pagans.

As with all sins, gluttony makes us solitary. Communion brings us together.

Gluttony teaches us to devour, while communion teaches us to savor. Communion reminds us how little it takes to be filled, while gluttony fills us with little but a desire for more. Meanwhile, the sponsored poets of advertising tell us, with fantastic allure, that food makes us happy. Why is it then that those who eat to be happy never are? Or that food taken as a substitute for sex and love ends up making us both less sexual and less lovable?

America's defining myth is that everyone can always have more, and should always want more. Watch a child on Christmas morning as he tears gleefully into the packages, scarcely able to enjoy one before ripping into another. Likewise we lurch between one meal and the next as if eating were the object of life. Overeating is even part of the landscape of tourism. Witness the offer made to any traveler near Amarillo, Texas, who will be given a free meal if he can consume a seventy-two-ounce steak in under an hour.

These images might not be so incongruent if we did not live in a world where countless children are starving. But we throw away enough food every day—scraping it off our suburban plates into our suburban disposals inside our suburban castles—to feed half the world. Now that we have declared a new war on terrorism, we should remember that it must be a war on poverty and hunger as well, because we will never be able to decapitate terrorists as fast as hunger breeds them. We also need to keep in mind that our addiction to oil, and the death-dealing lifestyle it makes possible, is but one more form of gluttony.

All of this makes the lively virtue of communion seem like more than just a good idea. Gluttony takes life. Communion gives life. Gluttony is the sad obsession of a hunger that is never satisfied. Communion is a way of making sure that part of us is never hungry again. Gluttony eats to feel better but ends up feeling worse. Communion eats to feel connected and ends up wanting nothing more. Gluttony is self-indulgent and sad. Communion gathers us into the company of sisters and brothers. Gluttony bends us over the trough. Communion straightens us up, makes us look each other in the eye, and say please and thank you.

Regarding our national obsession with dieting, I have a modest proposal: eat less, more often, with more friends. Take your mother's advice to chew slowly, and pause to speak and laugh with those at the table. You are likely to find that half the food, eaten with twice the love, satisfies three times as much.

Remember, a wisdom in your body discriminates between hunger and compulsion. You must feed both body and soul, and not assume that either one can completely satisfy the other. A hangover is God talking. The message is simple: You are gulping when you should be sipping.

A simple shared meal is the principal sacrament of human existence. We live around the table, and in sharing our lives, not just our bread, we are satisfied. Take. Eat. This is my body, broken for you. This is the bread of heaven; this is the cup of salvation. It isn't very much. But it is more than enough.

❦ ❦ ❦

*S*he used to go to the supermarket at three o'clock in the morning because nobody would see her then. Now she goes in the middle of the afternoon, when she needs groceries.

On this particular day, she slips past the checkout lanes, smiling and shaking her head as she passes the magazine rack, with its usual lineup of thin, buxom women mocking her with their perfect bodies, dangerous cleavage and come-hither looks. She knows the national motto: You can't be too rich or too thin.

Not true, *she thinks to herself.* Howard Hughes proved you can be too rich, and Karen Carpenter proved you can be too thin.

Moving past the candy, past the freezer full of ice cream, and beyond an entire aisle full of cookies, pastries and cake mixes, she comes at last to the bakery, which was her destination all along.

She is a deacon in her local church, and it's Saturday, and she is on a mission—to buy the bread for Holy Communion.

Looking at all the choices, she begins to wonder: What kind of bread is considered acceptable for Communion anyway? I mean, would God be just as happy with pumpernickel as with sourdough? And must it be brown, or could it be Wonder white, or Russian rye black?

Suddenly she realizes that the subject has never come up in a deacon's meeting, and now she must make a choice. Is everyone just supposed to know what Eucharistic bread looks like?

She settles on a nice, round, rough-looking loaf of wheat berry and puts it in her cart. One loaf, *she thinks,* will feed all two hundred of us. Just a pinch as the plate goes around, and a sip of wine from those little glass cups that take so long to fill and even longer to wash.

And yet, nobody will complain. They will take their share and hold it for as long as it takes for everyone to be served. The same with the cup. After the whole congregation has lifted those tiny cups and held them in their sweaty hands, the minister will pronounce it the cup of heaven, and all those heads will go back together.

Then, of course, comes one of the most distinctive of sanctuary sounds, the sound of all those cups being placed at once into the pew cup holders—the rippling, clicking sound of solidarity.

She lets her mind wander for a moment over days gone by. She had been diagnosed five years ago with an eating disorder, checked herself into the hospital and even considered having her stomach stapled. It was that or suicide, because she ate all the time in those days, for no reason—except that it was her one dependable pleasure.

When she checked out of the hospital, she made a decision that changed her whole life. She adopted a small child, a refugee whose plight was made known to her when she went on a mission trip to Nicaragua. This dark-haired girl, whose name was Maria, was all she thought about now. She thinks about her so often, in fact, that sometimes she forgets to eat.

The girl had almost died of malnutrition, and for months, the woman nursed her back to health, worrying all the time about whether she had the proper balance of calories, carbohydrates and starches.

The next morning, sitting in church, she looked at the loaf of brown bread on the Communion table and wondered again how it could possibly be enough. The words of institution were spoken. The bread was passed, and when everyone had partaken there was still some left over. She wasn't sure which was more miraculous— that it went all the way around or that she felt so full.

That night the two of them watched an old black-and-white movie. It was gauzy, romantic and therapeutically implausible. They made popcorn, and they laughed, and then, well before midnight, Maria fell fast asleep in her lap.

She carried Maria to bed, feeling the blessed weight of a sleeping child in her arms. She covered her up, smoothed her hair away from her face and then fell fast asleep beside her.

They both slept like a rock, and they both woke up hungry.

Chapter 6

WANTING WISELY,
NOT GREED

If money be not thy servant, it will be thy master.
The covetous man cannot so properly be said to
possess wealth, as that may be said to possess
him.

Francis Bacon

e was an orthopedic surgeon, a proud veteran of the Second World War, and a man who rightly claimed his place among what a recent book called the "greatest generation." Now seventy-eight and having lost his battle with diabetes, he was dying.

The good doctor had three sons, the oldest of whom became a multimillionaire when he pioneered the concept of selling blocks of long-distance time at a discount. He was in the right place at the right time, and after a few false starts the money came rolling in.

The surgeon father was a member of my parish and a good friend. I had officiated at his second marriage after his first wife died suddenly of a heart attack.

The eldest son also lost a wife, his second, to a brain tumor. I was asked to go to Tiberon, California, where they lived, to eulogize her. This is one of America's richest counties per capita, and it was like going to a different planet. I spoke to a congregation whose members were multimillionaires, not just millionaires, and it was the first time I had ever experienced so palpably the relationship between wealth and despair.

These people had everything, yet they seemed not just melancholy, but almost frantically insecure. They could buy anything, yet they seemed to enjoy nothing.

News about the eldest son came to me regularly from the father, and it was seldom good news. There had already been several divorces, and the newest wife, married on the rebound, had found another lover and left him. His children by a previous marriage had significant emotional and behavioral problems, and he was always trying to buy them love. He even looked into "renting" a wife and mother for them.

Meanwhile, the father was in his last days. Hospice had been called in, and my wife was making frequent visits to his bedside as a member of our church care-team. His other two sons had come to see him, but not the eldest—not the millionaire.

It dawned on all of us that before he could die, he wanted and needed to see his firstborn son. But the son never came. He kept saying he would come. But he never did.

That's when I learned that the son was a full-fledged alcoholic. He started drinking every day before noon, and he didn't stop until he passed out that night. I called him one morning at his palatial home in Denver and talked to the maid, who anxiously took the phone to him where he lay in a drunken stupor.

"Your father is dying," I said. "He needs to see you." In a thick and garbled tone of voice he agreed, saying he would get on a plane. We waited. He never came.

On the night his father died, the eldest son, who claimed repeatedly that he "just couldn't handle his father's death," was checked into an alcohol and drug rehabilitation unit, where he was still locked up on the morning we gathered in the sanctuary to honor his father's life. After failing to make it to the bedside, he managed to miss the funeral too—the most classic case of passive-aggressive avoidance I've ever seen.

This modern version of the prodigal son is becoming all too common. Unlike Luke's version, however, this son never came to his senses, never felt responsible before God. He never came home to show his love and ask for forgiveness. He not only stayed in the far country, but remained a captive there.

There was no robe, no ring, no sandals, no feast to mark the reunion. For unlike the biblical son who fell into poverty, and whose father rejoiced that his son was "dead and is now alive," the modern son, who fell into riches, never saw his father again, for he was alive but is now dead.

So too is the son. On the very day we scattered his father's ashes in San Francisco bay he overdosed on drugs and alcohol. His fourteen-year-old son found his father's corpse in bed, and he is now a lost son himself.

"Children of privilege," we call them.

☙ ☙ ☙

In preparing to preach a sermon on greed, I went to Blockbuster and rented the ultimate '80s movie on the subject—*Wall Street*, starring Michael Douglas as the infamous Gordon Gecko. Here is Hollywood's version of the deadly sin of greed, the very embodiment of avarice gone amok. Not in a mood to watch it all again, I simply fast-forwarded to the scene that I remembered so well from having watched it in a theater over a decade ago.

Gecko, the ultimate Wall Street bandit, is addressing a stockholders' meeting of a company called Teldar Paper. He is about to "save" it by "downsizing it." Suddenly, he launches into his own sermon, extolling the virtues of greed—something the church has called a deadly sin since the Middle Ages:

> Greed, for lack of a better word, is good. Greed is right. Greed works. Greed clarifies, cuts through and captures the essence of the evolutionary spirit. Greed, in all of its forms—greed for life, for money, for love, knowledge—has marked the upward surge of mankind, and greed, you mark my words, will not only save Teldar Paper, but that other malfunctioning corporation called the USA.

Douglas's was a riveting performance. It was also a case of art imitating life. I have now met countless people who live by this credo, who belong to the most materialistic generation ever raised in America. I live in a culture where greed is not just considered good. It is considered gospel.

Never mind that Enron was just the tip of the iceberg when it comes to the corporate crime wave sweeping America. Never mind that accountants are now in cahoots with the companies they are supposed to audit, insiders trade after hours, and millions of employees have been robbed of their pensions. Never mind that as companies go under, CEOs plead ignorance and walk away with what they've stolen and almost never go to jail.

In America, if you are homeless and rob a 7-11 you'll get ten years to life. But in corporate America, you can steal all you want and fly away untouched—in the first-class cabin, of course.

Getting anyone to talk about this is not easy, however. Money has been called the last taboo. We can talk about anything else—no matter how personal or shocking—but it is still considered unthinkable to discuss the money that someone else makes. Next to sex, we are more hypocritical about money than about anything else. We rail against the rich, and yet most of us would jump at the chance to trade places with them. "Come ye rich, weep and howl," says the author of the epistle of James. You can bet that was said to a poor congregation!

What's more, some truth underlies what the fictional Gecko says, even if we hate to admit it. Had he used the word "desire" instead of the word "greed," he might have been able to get away with it. The fact that human beings "want" things in life, beyond what they merely "need," is the engine that drives free enterprise, fuels creativity and makes sure that the nest is not just built, but feathered.

Our problem is not that we want things. Some things are worth wanting and waiting for. Desire is life's rawest form of energy, but the sad truth is that we are taught to want without limits. Enough is never enough. "Whoever dies with the most toys wins," mocks the bumper sticker. But that's no joke. Countless baby boomers have made the jump from "Make Love Not War" to "Image Is Everything."

Even though many of our excesses finally caught up with us when the stock bubble burst, we have all lived through a time of unparalleled prosperity. After the collapse of communism, we developed an almost religious devotion to the notion that the marketplace can solve all the problems of life. By default, we have reduced the idea of value to the most amoral of standards: whatever the market will bear.

What's good is what sells. Period. This concept has produced a culture that is often both rude and crude, and pits us against one another in a real-life game of Monopoly. What we have forgotten is that the unbridled excesses of capitalism are what gave birth to communism in the first place. Despite what Mr. Gecko says, unbridled greed is and has always been the foremost enemy of free enterprise. Gandhi was right when he said that capitalism without a conscience cannot survive.

The problem is that we don't know where to draw the line

between wanting things in an appropriate way and being consumed by greed. Perhaps a clear definition of greed is in order.

Greed is the inordinate love of money and material possessions, and the compulsive behavior that is driven by the need to have more and more of both. The truly greedy person is never content and is willing to sacrifice everything (and everyone) to acquire more. He can scarcely enjoy what he has for thinking always of what he wants.

Also known as "avarice" and "covetousness," greed manifests itself in many ways. The cutthroat competitor, the workaholic, the swindler, the miser and the gambler can all be greedy. Sometimes even the spendthrift is guilty of greed because his extravagance is just another form of selfishness.

Given that greed is a deadly sin—a destroyer of families, friends and even nations—you would think that the church would be preaching against it regularly. But alas, at just the moment in history when we need to preach against greed, we seem to have lost our homiletical nerve. When it comes to money, and making more and more of it, the church has joined in the hunt. So-called prosperity theology is everywhere, promising people they will get rich if they just invite Jesus into their lives.

This concept is very strange indeed, especially if you actually read the New Testament. Wealth wasn't considered a sin, but it was definitely considered to be spiritually debilitating. One seldom hears sermons today about the dangers of storing up treasures on earth, or about how difficult it is for a rich man to enter the kingdom of heaven. As for the impossibility of serving both God and mammon, this is a tough sell in churches that use one to serve the other.

Pulpits are full of linguistic blushes when it comes to the dangers of greed. We speak of "financial success," "economic security" or "the good life." The airwaves are full of televangelists whose principal appeal to their faceless audience is the possibility of instant riches—and they aren't talking about peace of mind or spiritual riches, mind you. They are telling people that God will reward their faithfulness by making them wealthy on earth. This involves an "initial investment," of course—a "seed gift" to the ministry. But with "sufficient faith" (more and bigger gifts), it will all come back tenfold.

Often those who do send in money are the least able to do so, but they are desperate. This is the ugly side of religion, the church itself consumed by greed instead of preaching against it. Not only are famous preachers now millionaires, but they use the trust and culpability of their congregations to build enormous edifices that resemble malls more than houses of worship. To justify their own wealth, they imply that their success is a sign from God that their message is true and their lives are righteous. The recent popularity of the Prayer of Jabez is a good example. Anyone who thinks that prayer is not about material wealth hasn't read it. And anyone who thinks the church is not a slave to greed hasn't visited a so-called megachurch lately.

From billboards to radio and television pitches, the message is clear: religion has become a kind of success strategy. It promises "victory," but not in the old-fashioned sense of freedom from the bondage of sin, or as an alternative to the worldly addiction to manna. Rather, this victory manifests itself in "financial independence" and a very tangible return on one's spiritual investment. Jesus warned people about worshiping money. The church is now helping people make it.

The truth is that we have all been caught up, at some level, in the notion that life is all about the pursuit of material wealth, that we are as we accumulate. After all, we idolize the rich. We study them and presume that something is extraordinary about them. We listen to them as if they are full of wisdom. We live vicariously through their conspicuous consumption.

In the American West, homes are being built that are only accessible by helicopter, so that rich people can vacation there for two weeks a year. At a recent wedding in an upscale megachurch in Oklahoma City, fifty thousand dollars were spent on flowers alone. But why not? This very church, like so many power-of-positive-thinking churches, blatantly mixes religion and material success—turning Jesus into a form of neutral energy.

The prophetic Jesus is out, and the cosmic friend and financial advisor is in. No longer a radically disturbing presence (asking the rich young ruler to sell all he had, give the money to the poor and follow him), the New Jesus is a kind of cosmic, life-enhancing partner. He has become an additive of sorts, like STP. You put him in your tank and get wherever you're going faster and with fewer knocks. Exactly where you're going doesn't seem to matter much.

A recent article in the *New York Times* reports that although Harvard University now has an endowment of $19 billion, it refuses to pay its janitors a living wage. You'd think that with all that brilliance concentrated in one place, somebody would be smart enough to suggest that in addition to being profoundly intellectual, they should also be decent.

Once, while riding in a car with a friend of mine who is a multimillionaire, I asked him to tell me what he wanted most in life. He said, without hesitation, "Thirty-two million more . . . that would make me happy." And he wasn't kidding.

No wonder St. Thomas Aquinas gave avarice first rank among the deadly seven as the "the root of all sins." Avarice is desire run amok, where what we need and what we want bear no relationship to each other. For others, it's the thrill of the chase after money that counts. It's like a game that involves skill, risk-taking and the exhilaration of victory when they succeed.

For others, avarice is the result of envy. People pursue wealth and the things that money can buy in order to assuage their feeling that they are less "successful" than others to whom they compare themselves.

Sometimes pressure comes from a spouse, who has a different idea of what being successful means. For still others, it is a way of trying to alleviate anxiety about future security. Often such a person is so anxious about the future that he mortgages the present in order to secure it.

Meanwhile, a recent TV program was called *Greed*, and one of the most highly rated game shows ever was called *Who Wants to Be a Millionaire?* The answer is obvious: everyone. The question is, when does the pursuit of wealth satisfy the real intent of the Protestant work ethic, and when does it become what one writer calls "toxic wealth" and medieval moralists called "spiritual dropsy"?

A quick surf through today's cable TV wasteland allows you to visit programs that promise get-rich schemes through no-down-payment real estate plans. They feature financial gurus who exude vitality and bliss at having made a million before they were thirty. Their commitment is not to hard work, virtue or fidelity to principle, but to beating the system. Gambling is epidemic in America, as is gambling addiction. At the root of this cancer is the hope that we will strike it rich; now the government gets into the act by promising help for education while perpetuating a cruel hoax against phenomenal odds: the lottery.

Never mind that actual lottery winners are a sorry lot whose lives are made worse, not better by instant wealth. That story would require real journalism, and today's media is in the entertainment business. All we see is the winner at

the door, her face beaming in disbelief as she yelps deliri-
ously and thanks God for answering her prayers. After the
prize patrol has pulled away from the house, she is transformed from a life of drudgery and boredom to one of
excitement and adventure.

If this exercise in delusion isn't bad enough, consider the
real lesson that the lottery teaches our children: You don't
succeed by hard work, discipline and sacrifice, but by getting
lucky!

How strange it is to turn fifty and see what has become of
my generation, who hummed along with the Beatles singing
"Can't Buy Me Love" and then became the most shamelessly
materialistic generation in history. Now it's "Just Do It," or my
favorite line from a hair color commercial: "It may be expensive, but I'm worth it."

Somewhere on the road between "Love Is All You Need"
and "Material Girl," we have lost the wisdom of Epicurus:
"Wealth consists not in having great possessions but in having few wants."

The problem is that we live in a society that tells us incessantly that we are born to shop and that consumption is the
object of life. Witness the sad spectacle on the Friday after
Thanksgiving every year. People stay up all night to be the
first in line at the discount stores. In the rush to be the first
to grab a cart and head down the aisle, people have been
trampled. Bargain hunters now commit acts of shopping
rage.

More and more, we seem to have lost the capacity to distinguish between what we need and what we want. That's not to say that everything we need is really essential, or that everything we want is really bad.

True needs are imperious. You have to have food, water and shelter. Desires, on the other hand, are optional. Strong desires may take on the psychological exigency of need, even to the point of sounding absurd: "I'll just die if I don't get that house!" But guess what? Not getting that house won't actually kill you.

What we need, from church and society alike, is a clearer understanding of when desire is good, even essential to elevating life beyond mere survival, and when it becomes an obsessive vice. What we need is a means of deciding whether we are WANTING WISELY, or just being greedy.

This decision is not as easy as it sounds because the line between strong desire and greed is notoriously gray. J. Philip Wogaman, a Christian ethicist, reminds us of the important distinction that philosophers make between intrinsic and instrumental values. Some things are valued because they are instrumental in acquiring something else. Others are valued in and of themselves. Our society has the tendency to treat human relationships and other intrinsic values as if they were instrumental ones, measurable in purely economic terms.

For example, friends ought to have intrinsic value. They should be of value in and of themselves, and not merely as means to an end. We have all been used by other people, and we know how it feels. Greed can cause us to sacrifice what's really important in order to obtain what really isn't. The expression, "It's lonely at the top" reveals more than we know. Part of the reason for that loneliness is that we have climbed over everyone else to get there and don't have any friends left.

Moral philosophers do not consider the pursuit of wealth as sinful, and the Bible does not label wealth as sinful or the wealthy as sinners. What matters is how that wealth was acquired, at what cost, for what purpose and to what end. What is considered sinful is the damage we do to others as we acquire more and more. More important is our failure to regard all blessings as having come from God and into our temporary custody to be managed and shared. Biblically speaking, being rich is not a sin, but being stingy is. The real problem with greed, as with so many other deadly sins, is that it is born of selfishness.

Aristotle applied his concept of the golden mean to our attitude toward money, calling it "liberality." This virtue, which is the center line between the vices of prodigality (extravagance) and illiberality (stinginess) is marked by the wise use of money. The liberal man, in Aristotle's definition, gives it to the right people, in the right amounts, on the appropriate occasions and for the right reasons. What's more, they do not easily become rich because they are not interested in retaining money for money's sake. They value it not for itself or the things it can buy, but for the uses to which it can be put, particularly through giving it to others.

Again we circle back to a root cause of all the deadly sins: idolatry. Something has taken the place of God and is being worshiped (literally) to death. Political parties worship their own golden calves. No matter how many times it is proven that trickle-down economics doesn't work, for example, we continue to act, in regular political cycles, as if it does. When we tried it in the 1980s, it hurt the middle class, and we quit for a while. As Ross Perot put it: "We threw a lot of money at the top in those days, and most of it stayed up there."

Before September 11, 2001, Congress passed into law a $1.35 trillion tax cut (nearly $4 trillion if left in place over twenty years), almost half of which will benefit the wealthiest 1 percent of Americans. Two more tax cuts have further widened the gap between rich and poor, and the result is the largest deficit in U.S. history. Wealth now buys power, which rewards wealth, which buys yet more power.

In a stunning reversal, the government, which used to act as a check upon greed, acting on behalf of the last and the least, now acts mostly on behalf of those who are the least needy! Politicians call it supply-side economics, with the benefits trickling down. Although this theory holds some truth, only a fine line separates economic theory and plain, old-fashioned greed.

And yet desire, even strong desire, is a gift from God. Can it ever be said that a man's strong desire to listen to Bach is "greedy?" A man who expands his business wisely, manages it well and prospers enough to send his kids to college and retire in comfort is not being greedy, is he? What about the mother who adds a nursery to her house to accommodate a new arrival? Is this not altogether different from the same woman adding onto her house so that it will be bigger than her neighbor's house?

The problem with a truly greedy person is that he or she loses a sense of proportionality. More is always better, even when it's not. Consumption becomes compulsion, and he cannot stop. What's more, everything gets turned into a commodity. When she sees beauty, she wants to buy it. The validity of an idea is based solely on its profit potential.

A greedy person's moods swing up and down with the market, and that's hard on everyone. When the market is down, he is depressed; when it's up, he worries about its inevitable decline. The more he accumulates, the more he hopes to become. But in fact he becomes less by never believing that he can ever have enough. Jeremy Taylor's old maxim holds true: "No wealth can satisfy the covetous desire for wealth."

A person who understands the virtue of wanting wisely, even when the desire is very strong, will set a goal that has intrinsic rather than idolatrous value. A father's desire to spend more time with his children, for example, can become a powerful form of wanting wisely, but it is not a symptom of greed, unless there is some unspoken contest in the neighborhood to see which father can spend the most time with his children.

Greed is always out to prove something. Wanting wisely seeks to change something for a good reason, not a purely selfish one. To purchase a cabin in the mountains and restore it may not be a sign that you are trying to prove anything to the world. Rather, it may simply mean that you love the mountains, and you want to have a place to get away and spend time with family.

If you want to distinguish between greed and wanting wisely, you can understand the value of buying an existing cabin, rather than cutting down more trees and gobbling up more land to claim your vacation spot. Restoration is one way to want things wisely. Suburban sprawl is a symptom of greed.

To want something wisely is to want it for reasons other than self-aggrandizement or status. A strong element of creativity is often present in that kind of desire, as when adults suddenly change careers, or take time to travel or finish a project. The desire that parents have to provide the best possible education for their children, if properly motivated, is a very wise kind of wanting indeed—and a very creative one as well. On the other hand, parents who put their children in the most elite and expensive private kindergartens not because it makes any sense, but in order that they will be on the fast track to fame and fortune are passing down the sin of greed.

Or take gardening. Wanting an English garden and working hard enough to have one is a wise and wonderful thing. If, however, upon learning that English gardens are "in," you have one installed at great expense, and then hire a gardener to make sure it's the envy of the neighborhood, you are being greedy.

One of the most amazing statistics about American real estate is that at any given moment one out of every four houses is unoccupied—and this in a land full of homeless people. As baby-boomers age, and their children leave home, we are not building smaller houses, but bigger ones. Square footage now has nothing to do with need and everything to do with status.

In fact, greed is perhaps most clearly evident in the way we use and occupy space. Observe carefully the way a man or woman occupies space, talks about space and reserves space for private use. Their actions speak volumes about the difference between wanting wisely and being greedy.

In the city where I live and do ministry the wealthiest neighborhood is called Nichols Hills. It is full of thirty-room mansions in which only two elderly people live. I imagine that it must take an elaborate intercom system for them to keep track of one another: "Hazel . . . come in. . . . I'm in the lower dining room. . . . Are you in bedroom fourteen or bathroom six?"

At some point, this lifestyle becomes obscene and immoral, yet we have no one who seems willing to say so.

No voice, not even that of the church, is willing to call greed a deadly sin again or to offer a more constructive alternative than moving to a monastery.

Let me illustrate how difficult this whole business of wanting wisely really is by offering an example that is bound to make some people nervous, if not hostile. My wife and I have decided to stop buying diamonds. We love them as much as anyone, and she is as much a victim of the "diamonds are a girl's best friend" mentality as the next woman. The problem is that we don't like what we know about how diamonds make it to market. We know that their scarcity is manufactured, and the process by which they are mined causes great suffering, funds tribal violence, and can lead to amputation and even death. We still find ourselves wanting diamonds, but we can no longer want them wisely.

These comments are not intended to mean that everyone who has or wants a diamond is greedy. At some point, though, the size and cost of the diamond become more important than any message of love, and that is greed. But wanting wisely is the direction in which we need to move because the simple truth is that we cannot continue to consume as unwisely as we do and not destroy the planet and thus ourselves.

I have spent twenty-five years in the ministry watching my wealthiest friends struggle with their souls, and it has mostly been a losing battle. Riches are not evil, but Jesus was clear about this: Wealth is spiritually hazardous.

"Sell what you have, give it to the poor, and come, follow me," Jesus said to the rich man who wanted to gain eternal life. But the rich man couldn't do it; he had many possessions. "How hard it is for those who have wealth to enter the kingdom of God! Indeed, it is easier for a camel to go through the eye of a needle than for someone who is rich to enter the kingdom of God."

Why is this so? Because the rich so often think of nothing else. Their preoccupation with wealth—making more, keeping more, and using it to ensure their status and power—squeezes out all the time and energy required to care for other people and show compassion. The prize upon which they constantly fix their gaze makes them blind to the needs of those around them and to the temporal nature of their riches. They are so busy making money that they have no time to make a life.

"From him to whom much is given, much will be expected." Why don't we ever hear a sermon on that text? Have we given the world a false dichotomy in demanding either voluntary poverty on the one hand or a lifetime of guilt on the other?

People who succeed in this world and become wealthy are not all immoral, but they all have a moral responsibility to give something back to the world from which their riches came.

Rich people are so indignant about paying taxes, and yet the civilization that has been created by those taxes is what

made them rich in the first place. A world with no redistrib-
uted wealth is a world without roads, schools, hospitals and
standing armies. It's a world without the infrastructure and
laws necessary for anyone to be a successful merchant. My
favorite road sign in Oklahoma is one demanding that we
pay no taxes—placed for maximum effect along a federally
funded interstate highway!

In the end, we all must remember that having money
proves nothing and confers no real value. Money is just a
portable form of power. Hoarding it is greedy. Spending it
wisely is a blessing.

In Judaism one is to use wealth "for the sake of heaven."
For Christians, the word is stewardship. Either way, knowing
what money is and what it is good for is a mark of religious
faith. Seeing how high you can stack it is pathetic. Giving it
away for the right reason is an act of faith. To put this in
terms of the story of Lazarus and the rich man, the consequences of great wealth that ignores desperate poverty are
all too obvious.

A rich man who dressed in purple and fine linen and "feasted
sumptuously every day" totally ignores a poor man named
Lazarus who lies at his gate covered with sores and hoping to
catch a few crumbs that might fall from the rich man's table.
They both die, but the poor man is carried away by angels to be
with Abraham. The rich man is tormented in Hades.

Looking up and seeing Abraham with Lazarus by his side,
the rich man begs for mercy, asking only to have Lazarus dip

the tip of his finger in water and cool off his tongue. But Abraham says:

> *Child, remember that during your lifetime you received your good things and Lazarus in like manner evil things; but now he is comforted here, and you are in agony. Besides all this, between you and us a great chasm has been fixed, so that those who might want to pass from here to you cannot do so, and no one can cross from there to us. (Luke 16:25–26)*

That "great chasm" describes the two worlds in which the very rich and the very poor live. They might as well be living in parallel universes. Great wealth creates a world so insulated, so protected, so luxurious that the rest of humanity is easily forgotten. Such is the source of a saying attributed to Marie Antoinette, who upon being told that her people had no bread, said, *"Qu'ils mangent de la brioche."* Let them eat cake.

Surely the gifts of this world are to be opened and enjoyed. Surely we were meant to want all manner of things wisely—for their own sake. But if we love money more than life, then we will lose both.

❧ ❧ ❧

He was an orthopedic surgeon, a proud veteran of the Second World War, and a man who rightly claimed his place among what a recent book called the "greatest generation." Now seventy-eight and having lost his battle with diabetes, he was dying.

The good doctor had three sons, the oldest of whom had become a multimillionaire when he pioneered the idea of selling blocks of long distance time at a discount. He was in the right place at the right time, and after a few false starts the money came rolling in.

The surgeon father was a member of my parish and a good friend. I had officiated at his second marriage after his first wife died suddenly of a heart attack.

The eldest son had also lost a wife, to a brain tumor, and I was asked to go to Tiberon, California, where they lived, to eulogize her. This is one of America's richest counties per capita, and for me it was like going to another planet. I spoke to a congregation whose members were multimillionaires, not just millionaires, and it was the first time I had ever experienced so palpably the relationship between wealth and despair.

These people had everything, yet they seemed not just melancholy, but almost frantically insecure. They could buy anything, yet they seemed to enjoy nothing.

All of them, that is, except the eldest son of the good doctor. He had been raised to believe that none of what he owned really belonged to him, and that in the face of all that life can bring us, both joy and sorrow, he would always be thankful and never give in to self-pity.

After his wife died, he made a mistake and married too quickly. His second wife had obviously married him for his money, and when she had an affair and left him, it broke his heart. For a time, it seemed as if everything was going wrong, but he still had his children, and they were a source of joy to him. He spent as much time as possible with them, and it's hard to say who needed whom the most.

When news about his father's illness reached him, he struggled to manage his business and make time for his father, but he knew which one was most important. He came to his father's bedside as soon as he could, and he spent many days there.

In his last days, the father, barely able to speak, and with his two other sons already at his side (for they had always been with him, and all that he had was theirs), saw his eldest son coming through the door, returning from a far country. If he could have gotten out of bed and run to meet him, he would have.

"I can die in peace now," the father said. "I have seen my immortality, and in your faces I can see your mother. Thank you all for being here. Thank you all for coming home."

He took several long, labored breaths, and then he breathed his last. What remained was nothing but a lump in the bedclothes, inert and eerily void.

But instead of sadness, there was a kind of deep, unspoken gratitude. For although the father was alive yet now is dead, the son was never lost.

Chapter 7

CONTENTMENT,
NOT SLOTH

When I consider how my light is spent
Ere half my days in this dark world and wide,
And that one talent which is death to hide
Lodged with me useless, though my soul more bent
To serve there with my Maker, and present
My true account, lest He returning chide.
"Doth God exact day-labor, light denied?"
I fondly ask. But Patience, to prevent
That murmur, soon replies, "God doth not need
Either man's work or his own gifts. Who best
Bear His mild yoke, they serve Him best . . .
They also serve who only stand and wait."

John Milton

$\mathfrak{H}$e was born a preacher's son, and what he remembers most about his father was the softness of his hands and the fact that he was never home. "Another committee meeting tonight," his mother would muse. "Saving someone, somewhere, at a distance that the minutes of the meeting won't do justice to."

After graduation from college, the son married and was accepted to Yale Divinity School, and his father was Ivy League–proud. "You have royal hands," he said, "and they will do royal work. Just promise me they won't be idle hands."

"But first I want to spend the summer at Ghost Ranch," his son announced.

"Where is that?" the father asked, sounding incredulous. "What is that?"

"It's a Presbyterian camp and conference center near Abiquiu, New Mexico," the son replied. "I went there on a youth group trip when I was in high school, and I've never forgotten it. There are red rock mesas that rise above a valley unchanged since the dinosaurs. And they say the light there is beyond describing.

Georgia O'Keeffe moved there to paint that light, and then never went home."

The father had heard of Georgia O'Keeffe.

"And what will you do there all summer?" he asked, still worried about idle hands.

"Work on service corps, at the farm perhaps—probably pulling weeds all day, or feeding the new lambs, or fixing something broken."

"And how will this prepare you for seminary?" the father asked, still worried about idle hands.

"I don't know, Dad. Maybe I just want to dig in the dirt a little bit before I started digging into the books." He thought this turn of phrase would please his father. It didn't. His father had a thing about idle hands.

"Sounds like a good way to waste the summer," his father said, "But do what you must. Just make sure you're home in time for orientation."

So the preacher's son went to Ghost Ranch, without a blessing from his father, and took his new wife with him. They spent the summer together pulling weeds, mending fences and feeding new lambs. By the end of the summer, his hands were rough, his face was brown, and his wife was pregnant.

Twenty-five years later they made him a bishop, and he came home late one night to give his family the news. He had not returned a single time to Ghost Ranch, heeding his father's advice about idle hands. There were, after all, meetings to attend, people to visit and a world to save. No time for idle hands.

Then one night, he came home to an empty house. A note from his wife's hand was Scotch-taped to the refrigerator: "The child we brought home from Ghost Ranch does not know you, and neither do I. Every night, it's another meeting, saving someone, somewhere, at a distance that the minutes of the meeting won't do justice to."

The note went on to say that she would be going to stay with her mother for a while, to "think things over." In the last line she wrote: "I miss that man with the rough hands."

❦ ❦ ❦

Ministers are looking sad these days. Many are clinically depressed. It's easy to pick them out of a crowd. Their posture is rounded over by unrequited idealism. Their faces are puffy and creased with disappointment. The fire is gone. So is the joy of finding life's purpose and speaking the truth, long since replaced by intellectual sarcasm and the safe haven that is theological cynicism.

Once they burned with passion for their work. Now they realize that their pension is small, their sermons are sounding cranky, and despite all their hard work the world is still

If they hear one more joke that begins, "A minister, a rabbi and God were out golfing one day . . . ," they will run screaming from the room. If they meet even one more well meaning pagan who says, upon finding out what they do for a living, "Well, I'd better watch my language . . ." they will immediately start cursing like a sailor.

If they must sit through one more church mission meeting during which someone says one more time that "Charity begins at home" (and ends there as well), or quotes the Seven Last Words of the Church ("We've never done it that way before"), and then abstains from voting on whether or not to feed the poor, it's bound to happen. Some cleric is going to go berserk. He is going to leap up on the table, strip naked and shout, "Here I am, wicked man! Gaze upon my depravity! For I am lost, just like you. Wretched, loathsome and foul—stinking up the nostrils of God!

"Yes, you may put that in the minutes."

Seriously, the psychic health of ministers is alarming. Divorce rates among the clergy are worse than the national average. Sexual abuse is not limited to priests, but runs throughout a church that remains deeply divided about how body and soul fit together. The ill-defined nature of the ministry in the modern age makes many male clergy in particular feel estranged from both the culture and themselves, emasculated and trivial.

What's more, perhaps no burden on earth is greater than the expectation that one will always be out there "doing good." No other profession puts you and your family so permanently on display in the proverbial glass jar. Those who pay us to be good are continually monitoring our goodness and basing next year's raise on it. Above all, we must stay busy, smile, pray at the drop of a hat and never appear too "human."

Idle hands are the devil's invention, we are told, and so ministers must keep moving and never appear "lazy." To that end we are taught in seminary to keep records verifying that we are not idle: the number of baptisms performed, funerals conducted, pastoral calls and hospital visits made, weddings officiated, counseling sessions held, confirmation classes taught. Because it's right there in the Bible: the numbers matter to God.

Besides, if you are in the world-saving business, you never have enough time, and the last thing you want to be called is slothful. Sloth is the last of the Seven Deadly Sins, and surely the most misunderstood.

To begin with, "sloth" is an archaic word. To the modern ear, it almost sounds quaint. Sloth sounds like a big furry creature to me—something that naps all day under a rock, or in a tree. The English word itself has long since been retired by lack of usage. It's gone to an Old Words nursing home where it commiserates about the good old days with other forgotten words, like "eschatology" and "transfiguration."

"Sloth" sounds like being lazy, like lying too long in the bathwater or sleeping through breakfast. But it hardly sounds deadly, certainly not like a capital offense.

Pride, envy, anger, lust and greed are things to worry about. But sloth? Does anyone preach sermons against sloth anymore? When was the last time you heard a TV evangelist railing against coach potatoes? As with gluttony, it is not politically correct to condemn what strikes most people as more unfortunate than deadly.

So it is that sloth limps along at the back of the pack of the Seven Deadly Sins. We cringe at most of them, but we wink at this one. We tend to consider it little more than an energy deficiency, and we counsel the offender to get out more or perhaps increase their caffeine consumption. After all, in a culture that admires leisure time as much as we do, the slothful may simply have decided to take it easy as a way of life.

Writers, of course, are considered the mavens of sloth. They are often asked to speak on the subject because of the common malady known as "writer's block"—an affliction known sometimes to resolve itself dramatically and without warning, much like constipation. One scholar even had fun with the idea that the slothful get together and commiserate. There are sloth symposia, sloth task forces and sloth hearings to help the perpetually slothful cope in the frenetic world of the hyperambitious. We aren't horrified by sloth here, we're laughing at it—or worse, we're laughing with it.

But wait a minute. Perhaps we find sloth harmless only because we have domesticated it and forgotten the original meaning of the word. In fact, sloth is a deadly and original meaning of the word. In fact, sloth is a deadly and death-dealing malaise, a spiritual stupor fed by apathy and resignation.

Sloth has two components: the Latin *acedia*, which means a lack of caring and an aimless indifference toward one's responsibilities to God and to humankind, and *tristitia*, meaning sadness or sorrow. On the surface, sloth looks like laziness. But underneath, and in its final stage, it is more than a physical condition. Sloth becomes despair at the possibility of salvation.

Sloth is not about deciding one morning that you will roll over and go back to sleep, or taking a nap in the afternoon when you should be painting the fence. Sloth is about a fundamental loss of faith in one's ability to do anything about anything. It is to live in a prison of apathy, rationalized through cynicism, where the favorite expressions are "So what?" and "I couldn't care less." Fred B. Craddock put it vividly:

It's the ability to look at a starving child, curled up in front of a store window with a swollen stomach and say, "Well, it's not my kid." To look at a recent widow, huddled under a gray shawl and peering out at a gray world, and say, "It's not my mom." Or to see an old man sitting alone among the pigeons in the park and say, "Well . . . that's not my dad." It is that capacity of the human spirit to look out upon the world and everything God made and say, I DON'T CARE.

Sloth is more than a cartoon of the coach potato. It's a sickness of the soul that leads to complete and utter indifference. Sloth was recognized as a grave sin by the Egyptian monastic desert communities of the fourth and fifth centuries. Monks would commonly become fatigued, bored and listless in their cells at midday. In their torpor they would experience "evil" thoughts that made them want to flee their monastic life, so it wasn't simply a lack of activity that made them slothful, but a turning away from duty, a loss of will.

Sociologists call the modern version of this widespread anguish anomie, alienation or despair. It is the most common complaint heard from the couch of the psychotherapist from patients who no longer feel that their lives have meaning or purpose. Life has become, they say, "sound and fury, signifying nothing." So why bother?

Matthew Arnold captured the real enemy of life's later years in his poem "Dover Beach":

> *Ah, love, let us be true*
> *To one another! For the world, which seems*
> *To lie before us like a land of dreams*
> *So various, so beautiful, so new,*
> *Hath really neither joy, nor love, nor light,*
> *Nor certitude, nor peace, nor help for pain;*
> *And we are here as on a darkling plain*
> *Swept with confused alarms of struggle and flight,*
> *Where ignorant armies clash by night.*

The truth is that as one grows older, the real enemy in life is despair. Kierkegaard called it the "sickness unto death." Our human tendency is to want to "secure ourselves against our own insecurity."

Because we are the only animal that is aware of its own mortality, we are prone to feeling that all we do is ultimately futile. Philosophers call it "angst," or "ontological shock." The bumper sticker says in the vernacular of our time "Life is tough, and then you die."

In response to the pressure we all feel to succeed and be recognized, some have decided to become nihilists who sleep until noon and then explain that rising early has no real merit, because, after all, the concept of merit is meaningless, given that we all die.

Perhaps this is just a reaction against the Protestant work ethic and the pressure put on us to do more, make more, be more. But this loss of spiritual moorings, and the ensuing vacuum that manifests itself in despondency and flight from the worship of God and service to others, is epidemic in our time.

Guilt over not accomplishing enough in life is a powerful force in American culture, and it has been from the very beginning. In his *Autobiography,* Ben Franklin confessed to allowing himself to sleep only from 1 A.M. to 5 A.M., after another four-hour block of nonwork time from 9 P.M. to 1 A.M., devoted to the "Evening Question, 'What good have I done this day?'"

Come to think of it, such a compulsive work ethic can actually pull the teeth of the other deadly sins. Pride can be dressed up as the "self-confidence to succeed"; envy as the motive for building a "better mouse trap"; anger as "giving people a piece of our minds"; lust as "sowing wild oats"; gluttony as an "admirable appetite for the best"; and greed as "entrepreneurial ambition." Finally, rendering sloth as nothing more than an annoying kind of lethargy applicable to the losers in life, the pat phrases become "get a move on . . . the day's half gone!"

Meanwhile, in the real world, millions of people are moving through life like zombies, staying outwardly busy but not finding anything much worth living for. But the purpose of life is to find meaning and to live that meaning. Viktor Frankl, author of *Man's Search for Meaning*, placed this responsibility squarely on each of us. He argued that no human being should ask what the meaning of life is, but must recognize that it is each of us who is asked, and we can only answer with our own lives. We do not question life, but rather life questions us.

The founder of logotherapy, a form of existential therapy that emphasizes the role of meaning in survival, Frankl would have been keenly aware of the sin of sloth because the responsibility to find and live a meaningful life requires active engagement and choice. He even went so far as to define a "neurotic" as someone who has failed at this task, whether for want of trying or for lack of success.

Carl Jung recognized the role of meaning in life as well, and the danger of thinking that it could come to us as passive recipients. In his now famous quote about the roots of despair in his older patients, Jung speaks without apology about the vital role of religion:

Among all my patients in the second half of life—that is to say, over thirty-five—there has not been one whose problem in the last resort was not that of finding a religious outlook on life. It is safe to say that every one of them fell ill because he had lost what the living religions of every age have given to their followers, and none of them has been really healed who did not regain his religious outlook.

While the least understood of the Seven Deadly Sins, sloth is also the most overtly religious in nature. The other six, although imbued with theological assumptions, are easily comprehended by the most secular among us as vices or significant defects. We can and do define anger, envy, gluttony, pride, greed and lust without reference to God. But the uniquely religious quality of sloth is evident in the fact that the Greco-Roman philosophers dealt extensively with the other six, but paid little attention to sloth. It took Judaism and Christianity to link this condition to the resistance of humankind to divinely imposed obligations.

As you might expect, the church came up with an "opposing" virtue and recommended zeal. This virtue is characterized by joy and steadfastness in the performance of religious and moral duties. The only problem is, nobody I know can be devoted to good works all the time and stay sane. Hence, they can be neither steadfast nor joyful—at least not all the time.

In fact, the illusion of the first makes the lack of the second inevitable. After all, no less a scholar than Martin Luther discovered, after praying fifty times a day and sleeping on nails night after night lest he become too "comfortable," that all his devotion did not add up to joy. Works alone, no matter how many or how well-intended, do not justify us.

Besides, let's be honest. In the church, we call perpetual do-gooders "busybodies," and they are the last people we would ever invite to a party. They are "world-savers," and the sins they attack are legion, but always far from home. Like the Dickens character from *Bleak House,* Mrs. Jellyby, they seem unable to recognize a problem closer to home than Africa, and thus they commit a sin the novelist calls "telescopic philanthropy." They are so busy righting wrongs and saving souls that they forget to pick up the milk, change the diapers or remember the whereabouts of their own lost children.

In our search for lively virtues that do not stare across an abyss at the deadly sins they oppose, but rise up out of our own flesh and blood, let's recommend one more. While the last, it is by no means the least. The seventh and final lively virtue is CONTENTMENT.

If there is a more important virtue for the world to recover than contentment, I'd like to know what it is. Perhaps you prefer the biblical phrase "peace of mind," but remember, Paul said, "I try, in whatever circumstance I find myself, to be content."

Contentment is not just an "peaceful, easy feeling" or a way to rationalize laziness. It is a deep, easy-breathing wisdom that knows what can and can't be changed, and more important, knows when to do and when to wait. The contented person watches the world closely, but does not stare it down. She enjoys things, rather than trying to possess them or straighten them out.

Some people are driven crazy by the repetitive futility of everyday chores. We water the grass so it will grow. Then we cut it and water it again, so it will grow, so we can cut it again. Meals are made, dishes are done, and then it's mealtime again. We dirty the dishes we just washed so we can wash the dishes we just dirtied, and one is tempted from time to time to let one fly across the kitchen.

But for other people, those chores only serve as a backdrop to contemplation. They are the Muzak, not the symphony score of their days. For just as we think of things in the car when driving long distances, mesmerized by the dashes of the center line as they disappear strobelike under the hood, so too can we do our most pedestrian tasks without feeling pedestrian. The dishes must be done, but they need not do us.

To be content in the religious sense requires perhaps the most difficult single attitude in the Western world: an almost mystical embrace of chaos. W. H. Auden called ours the "age of anxiety," and yet what does it mean to be anxious if not to experience the opposite of contentment? Anxiety comes not from uncertainty about the future (this is the human condition), but from believing that not enough is being done to change it. It comes from insecurity about ourselves and our basic self-worth. It is born in frustration at how little attention the world pays to us.

The contented person is not disengaged or laid back, but knows when and how to expend energy, and knows when it is being wasted. He still makes big plans and takes on important projects, but not at the expense of everyday moments, and especially not at the expense of the people he loves. He learns from failure, instead of being embittered by it, and he keeps all of his success in perspective.

A marvelous parable in the New Testament is often overlooked because it is so brief and appears so harmless. In Mark's Gospel, Jesus describes the kingdom of God as someone who scatters seed on the ground, "and [then] would sleep and rise night and day, and the seed would sprout and grow, he does not know how. The earth produces of itself, first the stalk, then the head, then the full grain in the head. But when the grain is ripe, at once he goes in with his sickle, because the harvest has come" (Mark 4:26–29).

In the ancient human dilemma of "when to do" and "when to wait," this parable not only answers the question, but defines the abiding characteristic of contentedness in terms of the proper order of things: first you do, then you wait. After you have done what only you can do (plant the seed), you wait while the seed does what only it can do. When the time for harvest has come, you gather in the crop that grew itself, but which cannot harvest itself.

The order here is very important. First the seed is sown, and now the sower knows that he can do nothing more so he waits. Nobody stands over a seed and screams, "Come on now, grow!" A seed carries its own future in its bosom. The sower has done all he can do. Now he waits patiently for God to do what only God can do.

No one would think to call his waiting slothful. It is wise. He turns his mind to other things. He hopes for rain. He mends fences. He watches and waits because he is not the master of the harvest, he is the steward of the mystery. When that mystery is fully present, his waiting is over, and he puts the sickle to the stalk.

Mark preserved this parable for an anxious church, one that waited for the return of Christ and wondered why it hadn't happened. The answer is that we cannot know, but that doesn't mean we shouldn't do what we can and then be content. We plant the seed of the word, and then we wait for the mysterious way in which God brings it to fullness. Fear not.

People seem very anxious these days, even more so since September 11. That dark day drove home a truth that we would rather not embrace: we are not able to control our world. We get no permanent exemption or special providence when it comes to senseless acts of violence. The age of innocence is gone.

But it goes deeper than this. Western culture has simultaneously preached an inherently contradictory message: look out for number one, but live in harmony with everything and everyone. Make sure you self-actualize by adopting yourself as life's primary project, but don't forget to sacrifice for others. Even the military establishment wants to have it both ways, as one of its new slogans quite ridiculously illustrates: BE AN ARMY OF ONE.

Perhaps this spiritual schizophrenia is responsible for much of the anxiety in the land, even that immobilizing apathy that deserves to be called sloth. To be content is not to ignore yourself entirely, nor to think that the world can't get along without you. It is to hold in tension two essentially religious ideas: that you are a child of God, infinitely precious, and that you, along with everyone else you know and love, are a sinner and have fallen short of God's intentions.

Knowing this, you neither retreat from making the world a better place nor assume that it can't happen without you. There is, after all, nothing quite as sad as a "bleeding heart" who does not know how or when to apply a tourniquet. For one thing, the blood would be better donated as plasma. For another, someone has to clean up the mess.

The contented person knows there are limits to what he or she can do, and yet this does not produce feelings of failure. It merely makes one more attentive to those moments when one can do something, and more patient in waiting for the harvest. The contented person trusts in what love can do when, once spoken, it bounces back from the canyon of time like a fivefold echo.

It is good to make grand plans, but a mistake to let them rob us of the joy of ordinary days. For many parents these days, zeal is just another word for being frantic. If we shuffle our children to enough events, drop them off at enough summer camps or deposit them for safe-keeping at enough vacation bible schools, they will come out on the other side not just short of breath, but full of virtue. Or so we hope. What they actually learn is that being busy does not mean being happy.

The contented man comes home from work and is present to his family. He doesn't just wink at them while talking on his cell phone, or go back to the office at night in order to show them how much he loves them. More stuff is not what they need. More time with their father is what they need. Part of being content is to leave undone that which by doing undoes us.

A contented person is comfortable with silence and does not use the TV for background noise. He does not eat quickly and hurry others along, because there is something more important to do. He does not cut vacations short to get home early and catch up at the office. He takes off his watch sometimes and is quite happy not knowing what time it is. He sips, instead of gulping. He takes no pleasure in what's wrong with the world, or in self-righteous complaining. Instead he is grateful that so much has gone well for him, compared to those who have less.

To care for the world, in fact, is to care for it wisely. And to care for it wisely is to care for it one person at a time, one moment at a time. Most of us will never yield great power and so our pronouncements about what's "wrong with the world today" or what's "wrong with kids today" or what's "wrong with schools today" will fall like sawdust onto a barroom floor: a pile of useless words, and sour ones at that. The next morning they will be swept up by the janitor whose job it is to dispose of what my grandmother called "leavings."

Besides, the harshest critics seldom lift a finger to change what they criticize. This point seems especially true of wealthy white males, who own most of the world yet complain incessantly that they don't own all of it. The seventeenth-century Puritan preacher Cotton Mather, who wrote *Bonifacious: An Essay upon the Good,* was fascinated by the idea of what would happen if successful men were as creative and ingenious in their religious and ethical lives as they are in their business endeavors. He devoted a whole chapter to "Rich Men," and charged them with a special responsibility to use their considerable means to alleviate suffering in the world. Of course, to do that they would have to quit whining.

The truth is, the world is full of well-intended people who want to change things, but have no idea how to do it. They offer daily prayers, they tithe and they work to be a model for their children, but something is missing. Quite frankly, for all their devotion, they do not seem happy. For all their committee work, they do not seem transformed. For all their talk about the blessed kingdom and the joy it brings, they seem never to have spent a single moment there. Like so many churchfolk, "joyful" is the last word that anyone would choose to describe them.

They are always in a hurry, always looking squint-eyed at something out of order, always analyzing and explaining the failure of others. Somewhere along the way they forgot the purpose of life itself, which is not just an endless striving toward perfection, but a gracious embrace of what is.

Contentment is not laziness or resignation. Contentment is the "peace that passes understanding." In the middle of the world's pain and sorrow, the contented person has perhaps the greatest lively virtue of them all. She is neither embittered, nor compulsive. She does what she can, planting a few seeds, and then waits upon that mysterious thing the ancients called "the fullness of time."

None of us should carry the burden of trying to save the world. It's not ours to save. And if we ever think that we can do enough good works to earn our way into heaven, then we will fall short of paradise, exhausted and full of despair. The purpose and end of human existence is captured in the shorter Westminster catechism: "To love God, and enjoy Him forever."

🦋 🦋 🦋

e was born a preacher's son, and what he remembers most about his father was the softness of his hands and the fact that he was never home. "Another committee meeting tonight," his mother would muse. "Saving someone, somewhere, at a distance that the minutes of the meeting won't do justice to."

After graduation from college, he married and was accepted to Yale Divinity School, and his father was Ivy League–proud. "You have royal hands," he said, "and they will do royal work. Just promise me they won't be idle hands."

"But first I want to spend the summer at Ghost Ranch," his son announced.

"Where is that?" the father asked, sounding incredulous. "What is that?"

"It's a Presbyterian camp and conference center near Abiquiu, New Mexico," the son replied. "I went there on a youth group trip

when I was in high school, and I've never forgotten it. There are red rock mesas that rise above a valley unchanged since the dinosaurs. And they say the light there is beyond describing. Georgia O'Keeffe moved there to paint that light and never went home."

The father had heard of Georgia O'Keeffe.

"And what will you do there all summer?" he asked, still worried about idle hands.

"Work on service corps, at the farm perhaps—probably pulling weeds all day, or feeding the new lambs, or fixing something broken."

"Sounds like a great idea," the father replied. "I can tell you, with some authority, that the life of the mind is a wonderful thing, but it's not enough. You need to keep your hands in the dirt, even if your head is in the clouds." The father was known to turn a phrase now and then.

So the young man went with his father's blessing, and he took his new wife with him. Together they spent the summer pulling weeds, mending fences and feeding the new lambs. By the end of the summer his hands were rough, his face was brown, and his wife was pregnant.

For the next twenty-five years, they went back every summer, no matter how busy he got with his parish. He went back because that's where his soul was, and where he felt closest to the Mystery.

At Ghost Ranch, they weren't the reverend and the missus. They were lovers soaking up the pale desert light and feeling time stand still as the sun moved across the rocks. When the moon rose over Kitchen Mesa it was time to go to bed. But in the middle of the *night they walked outside to discover that the stars had fallen down all over them.*

A second child came, and then a third, and they dragged each one along to this place that time forgot. By and by the young minister learned the wisdom of the Indians of the Southwest, who believe that the desert is a spiritual place because, in their words, "We are saved by the places that ignore us."

Ghost Ranch is no five-star hotel. It's a state of mind. And yet nowhere else on earth did this busy family feel so content.

One day it was announced that he would become a bishop. When he came home to give his family the news, they were all packing for another trip. His wife smiled and congratulated him, but she did not go on and on. Clerics get enough adulation, *she thought.*

"Hop in the car," she said. "We've got to get you to the ranch."

"What's the rush?" asked the Bishop-elect.

His wife looked at him and smiled.

"Your hands are too soft."

Epilogue:
Living the Seven Lively Virtues

None of us can ignore the basic human condition or pretend that we have been granted some special exemption from it. We are born selfish, and our entire journey is spent thinking mostly of ourselves. From a squawking bundle of need in the crib to our brittle and dim-eyed dance with death, we live mostly at the center of our own universe. Left unchecked and untreated, selfishness is the real mother and father of all human sin. The Seven Deadly Sins are the most famous wayward children, but human cruelty can take many forms.

There is an antidote to selfishness, however, and we call it virtue. Humans have this in their DNA as well, and it can make us empathic, compassionate and heroic. Instead of lists of rules to follow, virtue is bred from the habits of a lifetime. Virtue is measured by the capacities of character and conscience. The man or woman who wants to live the Seven Lively Virtues must know that they are more than ideas. They are a way of life.

You can recognize a virtuous person, for example, because he knows that the real root of the deadly sin of pride is insecurity. Most proud and arrogant behavior is compensatory and rooted in deep misgivings about one's true value. A man who knows that he is worthy, however, because human life itself is worthy, will have a deep reservoir of living water on which to draw.

He will not need to be the center of attention, because he has been attentive to his own center. He will not be impatient with mediocrity, or feel the need to control others, because he recognizes the worthiness of all human beings, as well as the universal desire for freedom. He does not feel entitled to a certain lifestyle, nor does he assume that he alone is righteous, because healthy self-love makes him cooperative and gracious.

You will recognize him because he isn't out to be recognized. He listens, because this is how you respect the worthiness of others. He neither dotes on himself like a spoiled child, nor fails to tend his own soul. He is on good terms with himself, and he does not judge what he does not understand. He grows old gracefully because looking young is not what makes him feel worthy. He carries himself lightly because he has nothing to prove. He is self-assured but never egotistical. He does not earn his worthiness, because he knows it's a gift. He wakes up every morning knowing exactly what he is: a child of God.

Every woman knows the sin of envy because she has looked upon another woman who is more beautiful and felt the green-eyed monster rising in her throat. Envy is always destructive because it wants to tear down what it cannot have. But there is a virtue called emulation that is not destructive at all. It sees beauty and is amazed by it. It sees truth and wants to become more truthful. It sees talent and wants to become more talented.

A woman who emulates those she admires does not try to imitate them. She allows herself to be instructed by them. She does not wish to replace the teacher, but only to be a worthy student and thus to teach others. If she is a mother, she knows that her children may envy her at first, but they will grow to emulate her later—for envy is about power, and emulation is about goodness.

In all things she will be wide-eyed and not squint-eyed. She will enjoy the good fortune of others and not resent it, and in so doing her own joy will only increase. Emulation is a vicarious way of life that embraces the virtue of others until some of it is left clinging to us like the white hairs of a cat against a black sweater. The woman who emulates those she admires becomes more like them—but not to replace them. She wants to be among their numbers and be enrolled in their class forever.

Every man who has ever made of fool of himself by explosive anger knows that it is consumptive and useless. Selfish anger in particular is the stuff of the playground. It nurses wounds, real or imagined, until vengeance becomes a sickness, and the childish game of getting even is a downward spiral.

But the man who knows the virtue of righteous indignation is possessed of a right wrath that can change the world. It is anger on behalf of others, rather than anger in service to himself, that fills him with rage and propels him into the courts of change. He is not burned up like a fool. He is indignant over the avoidable harm that is done to others because ethics is too often a parlor game instead of a protest march.

He can be recognized as a community organizer, a friend to the poor, and a defender of people without power and status. He supports the cause of others, giving his money anonymously and his time without fanfare. He is the leaven in the loaf of social change, and he values results more than publicity. He volunteers to serve on the school board because it is easy to complain, and even easier to withdraw into a life of private ambition. He is mad for all the right reasons, and he knows when to shout and when to whisper.

The man or woman who is consumed with lust, who forgets the unspoken promises that bodies make when they lie together, will bring heartache and tragedy to those they consume for their own pleasure. Sexual desire is both powerful and sublime, but it can destroy what it betrays and bring death into the courts of life and love. Nothing is as pure or as corruptible.

But the man or woman who has tasted holy eros will not confuse raw desire with virtue. Rather, they will know that virtue releases desire from its back-alley ways and brings it into the bed of the beloved with the most powerful erotic companion of all: trust. Such a man or woman does not trade heat for light, as if only the illicit can be sublime.

He does not taker his lover for granted. She does not use sex for favors. He is considerate and thoughtful, knowing that physical attraction is rooted in emotional intimacy and tangible tenderness. She remembers what attracted her to her lover in the first place and does not forget to keep the fires burning by being playful, empathic and adventuresome. Those who drink from the cup of holy eros borrow wine from the vineyards of heaven. But they know with whom to drink, and with whom it is right to be intoxicated.

The woman who lives to eat, instead of eating to live, commits the deadly sin of gluttony. Her name is legion, and together with countless obese men she withdraws into a shadowy world of consumption without conscience that has become a national epidemic. In a world that glorifies food and serves it up fast and fatty, gluttony has its roots in lone-liness and low self-esteem. Food makes promises it cannot keep, and we suffer the consequences of idolizing our belly.

But the woman who has acquired the virtue of commun-ion knows that food is not the object of eating. The people with whom we eat, and the gratitude with which we share the gift of food, is what turns a meal into a sacrament. Like any good thing, too much is not good, and bad manners are a symptom of selfishness. To commune with food and friends is to know that one can have too much of the former and too few of the latter. Communion is food that has been transformed by love into life.

The woman who knows the virtue of communion is not concerned with the next meal, but with the next moment. Food is a gift, first to her and then to those who sit at her table. It is not a contest, nor is it competition. It does not prove her love, but makes it manifest in conversation, in sharing and in moderation. She does not preside over a trough, but is the mistress of the table. Her rules are simple: Stop chewing before you speak, and stop eating when you are full. But most of all, eat to live, instead of living to eat.

The man who never has enough and thinks that the object of life is to get rich and stay rich by any means necessary until the day he dies is guilty of greed. When the history of the late twentieth and early twenty-first centuries is written, greed may well be remembered as the dominant character-istic of our age. No longer burdened by even a twinge of guilt over their great wealth in a world of want, today's billionaires do less good with their money than their philanthropist fathers; they give less to charity than America's beleaguered middle class. The gap between rich and poor has never been wider, nor grown faster.

But the man who embraces the virtue of wanting wisely knows that desire is both a blessing and a curse. Wanting things is not a sin, especially if those things are means to an end, not an end unto themselves. To want the best education for one's children, a comfortable home or a secure retirement are not manifestations of evil, but these things must serve a larger purpose than money for money's sake and status in a materialistic age.

The man who wants wisely will be recognized for his love of life, not for his love of things. He will save in order to be secure, not to outdo his neighbor. He will buy things that are functional, necessary and reasonable instead of impractical, unnecessary and obscenely expensive. He will recycle, he will give to charity, and he will buy a house based on his needs, not on his ego. But most of all, he will keep in proper perspective money and all it can buy. He will not serve money. Money will serve him.

Finally, the woman who has given up on life itself, who falls back into bed every morning convinced that nothing matters, that all energy expended on behalf of others is wasted energy, is guilty of the sin of sloth. This deadly malaise converts all hope into cynicism, all joy into lethargy, all faith into wishful thinking. It snores through the sympathy. It stays in pajamas all day. It rejects the wonder and goodness of everything God has made by saying, "Who cares?"

But the woman who has learned the virtue of content-ment knows that the opposite of sloth is not hyperactivity. To avoid sloth, she need not become a busybody. In fact, that way lies burnout and the sacrifice of one's family and one's soul on the altar of saving the world. To be content, she knows, means doing what you can, and then letting some things be. She knows that to be of any use to anyone, she must be good to herself as well.

You can recognize the woman who is content because she lives comfortably inside her own skin. She can stay home and read a good book and not think that the world will come to an end. She can be quiet because she respects silence, and she can rest from her own good works because she knows she does not work alone. She plants seeds, and then she waits, knowing that the farming is her job, but the harvest is up to God. She is far from lazy, but she also knows to care for herself so she can care for others. She has a quality that the world needs desperately just now. She has the "peace that passes all understanding."

For all their Hollywood glamour, the Seven Deadly Sins are really just seven fallen angels. Worthiness is the quiet, unspoken antidote to pride; emulation, not envy is what makes us all students of beauty and truth; righteous indignation is how we turn self-serving anger into a passion for change; holy eros, not lust, is how we keep monogamy from becoming monotonous; communion, not gluttony is how food becomes fellowship; wanting wisely, not greed, is how desire gets bent into useful shapes; and contentment, not sloth, is how we let it be, and trust the universe to unfold as it should.

Out with the Seven Deadly Sins, and in with the Seven
Lively Virtues. Go in peace, pray for peace, and love one
another.

Since 1985, Dr. Robin Meyers has been the Senior Minister of Mayflower Congregational UCC Church of Oklahoma City, the fastest growing UCC church in the Kansas/Oklahoma Conference. He is also Professor of Rhetoric in the Philosophy Department at Oklahoma City University, where he has taught since 1991.

A graduate of Wichita State University and Phillips Graduate Seminary, Dr. Meyers received a Doctor of Ministry degree from Drew University and a Ph.D. in Rhetoric from the Communication Department at the University of Oklahoma.

He is the author of two previous books, *With Ears to Hear: Preaching as Self-Persuasion* (Pilgrim Press, 1993), and *Morning Sun on a White Piano: Simple Pleasures and the Sacramental Life* (Doubleday, 1998).

Dr. Meyers was a finalist for the pulpit of the Riverside Church, the Earl Preacher at the Earl Lectures at Berkeley, the winner of the Angie Debo Civil Libertarian of the Year Award, and is a regular columnist for the *Oklahoma Gazette*, where he holds the record for most angry letters to the editor.

His Sunday sermon broadcast, *A Second Opinion on Christianity*, reaches thousands of Oklahomans who are searching for a more inclusive, less dogmatic faith. He is married to Shawn Meyers, an Oklahoma City sculptor, and they are the parents of three children, Blue, Chelsea, and Cass.